FREE CAMPGROUNDS
OF WASHINGTON & OREGON

Other books by KiKi Canniff

SAUVIE ISLAND
   A STEP BACK IN TIME

OREGON FREE
   A GUIDE TO THE BEST OF THE STATE'S
   COST FREE ATTRACTIONS

WASHINGTON FREE
   A GUIDE TO THE BEST OF THE STATE'S
   COST FREE ATTRACTIONS

FREE CAMPGROUNDS
OF WASHINGTON AND OREGON

By KiKi Canniff

Illustration by Janora Bayot.

Ki² Enterprises
P.O. Box 13322
Portland, Oregon 97213

Original © 1985
by
KiKi Canniff

Library of Congress Cataloging in Publication Data

Canniff, KiKi, 1948–
    Free campgrounds of Washington & Oregon.

    Includes index.
    1. Camp sites, facilities, etc.--Washington (State)--
Directories. 2. Camp sites, facilities, etc.--Oregon--
Directories. I. Title.
GV191.42.W2C35 1985   917.9704'43'025   85-8161
ISBN 0-9608744-4-5

ISBN #0-9608744-4-5

Ki² Enterprises
P.O. Box 13322
Portland, Oregon 97213

TABLE OF CONTENTS

INTRODUCTION

The main attraction for free campgrounds in Oregon and Washington is not necessarily their cost free status. Many exist in less trampled areas where you will find easy access to spectacular scenery, hiking trails, fishing and a chance to enjoy and study nature.

Camping restores the spirit. Cares seem to evaporate on the wind when exposed to the fresh air, open spaces and gentle sounds of the natural surroundings. Coping with near primitive conditions also brings a feeling of self-reliance to all and for youngsters a real, special knowledge of conservation and a love for wildlife and the land it calls home.

These two beautiful Pacific Northwest states offer a variety of landscapes. You may choose to camp in the woods or a mountain meadow, beside a lazy river, rushing stream, or in the open desert. Rugged canyons, quiet islands, lake shores and wilderness areas can be home for the night as well.

Whether you choose to sleep beneath the stars, in a tent or in the comfort of a recreational vehicle there's a spot just right for you. You may want to camp in one spot for the entire time or visit several campgrounds over an extended period of time.

Most of the campgrounds listed here have picnic tables, fire rings, water and toilet facilities. Those located near sea level open earlier (April) and remain open later (November) than those found at higher elevations. Spring arrives later in the mountains and with it a carpet of wildflowers. Blueberries, blackberries, strawberries, rose hips, wild vegetables and mushrooms are abundant in many areas later in the year.

In Oregon you can actually camp within the famed Great Basin. You'll find part of its northern portion in the state's southeastern corner. This is a stark, wilderness landscape of mountains and high desert country.

Oregon's northeastern corner offers mountainous campsites in an area nicknamed "Little Switzerland". Here you'll be awed by 126 towering mountain peaks, all over 8,000 feet high and some nearly 10,000 feet, 11 glacially carved canyons, 150 lakes and a full range of campground facilities.

The central portion of the state offers hot, dry desert, volcanic remains, crisp mountain air and beautiful scenery while the Cascade Mountain Range is dotted with campgrounds from border to border.

Although you'll find fewer free campgrounds in Oregon west of the I-5 corridor and along the coast, some do exist. Those have been included herein as well but are often filled up by late afternoon so plan on stopping early.

In Washington you can set up camp in a true rain forest. Giant spruce trees 300' tall, draped with moss, and the largest variety of wild mushrooms in the continental United States can be found near Forks.

Some of the smaller San Juan Islands, northwest of Seattle, are covered entirely by state parks. These offer boaters campsites where lush greenery is surrounded by sparkling blue waters. Granite Falls, Darrington, Concrete and Marblemount offer campsites for land bound enthusiasts aong with Bald Eagle nesting areas, ice caves, wild and scenic rivers, and hiking trails. The state's southern portion of the Cascade Mountain Range is dotted with free campsites too.

Washington's entire northeastern corner is a haven for those who love the outdoors. Caves, ghost towns, fishing, historic sites and hiking trails provide daytime entertainment. The state's southeastern corner was once winter camp to the Nez Perce Indians and is as appealing to campers today as it must have been to those Indians for centuries past.

Campgrounds that do not charge generally receive less maintenance than charging campgrounds. As long as each visitor leaves a clean camp, taking their garbage out with them, we can be assured these camps will remain open. Do not throw garbage down outhouse holes or future campers will soon be without facilities.

When toilet facilities are not available body wastes should be treated in much the same way a cat uses sand. Dig a shallow hole, 6" is plenty deep, and cover your waste, including toilet paper, with dirt. Stomp the dirt down firmly.

If piped or well water is not available you should boil lake water for 5 minutes before consuming. Most campers consider streams that rush over 30' or more of rocks and sand to be clean enough to drink. When in doubt boil or add Halazone tablets.

Campfires should be built in fire rings when available. At times the woods become dry and untended fires are extremely dangerous. If no fire ring is available select an area away from brush and overhanging branches and clear the land down to mineral soil. When breaking camp all fires should be stirred up and sprinkled heavily with water. If you hesitate to stick your hand into last nights ashes it's not out well enough to leave.

A good portion of the campgrounds listed here are managed by the U.S. Forest Service and Bureau of Land Management (BLM). Detailed maps can be obtained from both which clearly show roads, trails, lakes, rivers and streams. You can stop at any area BLM or Forest Service office for a look at their display copy or, for a small charge, you can purchase your own. This will make finding the campground easier and let you know exactly what can be found nearby.

If you are unable to find available campsites on Forest Service or BLM land you still have one free alternative left. As long as you choose a spot that is at least 100 yards from any body of water or developed campground, and it is not posted otherwise, you can set up camp. If you build a fire you must use caution when selecting its site and are required to have a shovel and a bucket handy. Bury all body wastes, pack out your garbage and return your temporary campsite to its original condition or better and no one will chase you away.

Remember too, for every free campground listed here 4-5 pay campgrounds exist. Many offer showers and electrical hookups, yet few can compete with the natural surroundings you'll find in **Free Campgrounds of Washington & Oregon.**

Happy travels,

KiKi Canniff

HOW TO USE THIS BOOK

This book is designed to be used in conjunction with an Oregon/ Washington state highway map. A small map of each state has been provided to give you the general location of each city. All of these cities shown on these two maps offer nearby free campgrounds.

The campgrounds are then grouped together by city. Each listing begins with the campground name and agency by which it is operated. The next line will tell you what facilities are available. Since most have toilet and water facilities these generally are not mentioned. Directions to the campgrounds always begin at the city line and are simply stated. FSR has been substituted for Forest Service Road and Cty for County Road.

WASHINGTON

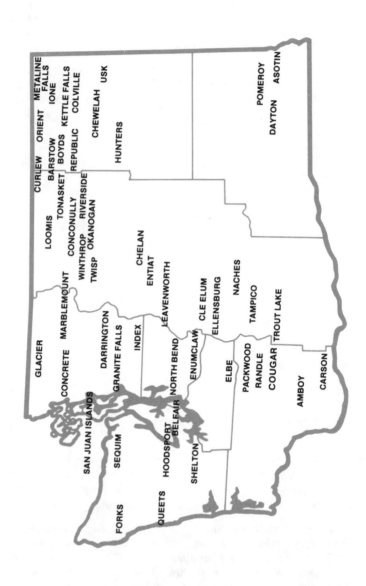

OREGON

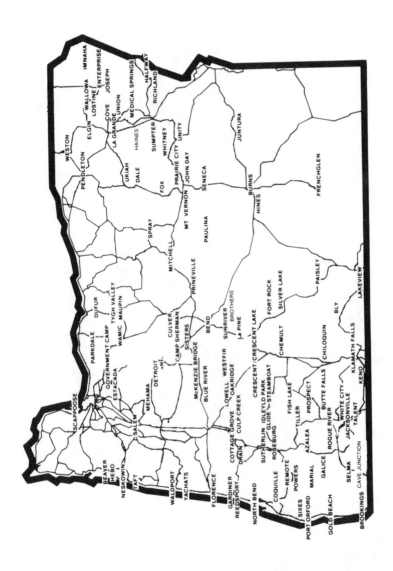

WASHINGTON CAMPGROUNDS

AMBOY

CANYON CREEK (Gifford Pinchot National Forest)
16 units, trailers to 18'.
East of Amboy. State 503 4.0 miles east, FSR 54 4.0 miles east, FSR 37 2.0 miles east.

ASOTIN

WICKIUP (Umatilla National Forest)
9 units, trailers to 18', piped water.
Southwest of Asotin. Cty 105 24.0 miles southwest. FSR 4300 7.0 miles southwest.

BARSTOW

ELBOW LAKE (Colville National Forest)
5 units, trailers to 18', well.
Northeast of Barstow. Cty 1500 12.0 miles north, FSR 1500 10.0 miles east.

BELFAIR

ALDRICH LAKE (Dept. of Natural Resources)
4 campsites, drinking water, trail, boat launch, fishing.
West of Belfair. Take Hwy 300 southwest approximately 13 miles to Maggie Lake Road. Turn right, follow to Dewatto Road and turn left. This will lead to Aldrich Lake if you stay left at the Y.

CAMP SPILLMAN (Dept. of Natural Resources)
6 campsites, drinking water, trail, fishing.
Northwest of Belfair. Leave Belfair heading southwest on Hwy 300 approximately 1 mile and turn right on Sandhill Road. At the Y take Goat Ranch Road to the left. The third road on the right leads to the campground.

GREEN MOUNTAIN HORSE CAMP (Dept. of Natural Resources)
9 campsites, drinking water, trail, horse facilities.
North of Belfair. Leave Belfair heading southwest on Hwy 300 approximately 1 mile and turn right on Sandhill Road. Stay right at the Y an additional 8 miles to Green Mountain Road. This will lead to the campground.

HOWELL LAKE (Dept. of Natural Resources)
6 campsites, drinking water, trail, boat launch, fishing.
West of Belfair. Take Hwy 300 southwest approximately 4 miles and turn right on Haven Lake Road. Stay left at the Y and follow to Howell Lake.

TAHUYA RIVER HORSE CAMP (Dept. of Natural Resources)
9 units, drinking water, fishing, trails, horse facilities.
Northwest of Belfair. leave Belfair heading southwest on Hwy 300 approximately 1 mile and turn right on Sandhill Road. At the Y take Goat Ranch Road to the left. The second road on the left leads to the campground.

TOONERVILLE (Dept. of Natural Resources)
4 campsites, trail.
Northwest of Belfair. Leave Belfair heading southwest on Hwy 300 approximately 1 mile and turn right on Sandhill Road. At the Y take Goat Ranch Road to the left. The first road on the right leads you 3-4 miles to the campground.

TWIN LAKES (Dept. of Natural Resources)
6 campsites, trail, boat launch, fishing.
Northwest of Belfair. Leave Belfair heading southwest on Hwy 300 approximately 1 mile and turn right on Sandhill Road. At the Y take Goat Ranch Road to the left, the fourth road on the right leads to the campground.

BOYDS

DAVIS LAKE (Colville National Forest)
4 units, trailers to 18', boat launch, fishing.
Northwest of Boyds. US 395 .5 miles north, FSR 9500 8.0 miles northwest.

CARSON

CREST (Gifford Pinchot National Forest)
3 units, trailers to 18', no water, Pacific Crest Trail.
Northwest of Carson. Cty 92135 4.5 miles northwest, Cty 21390 1.0 mile northwest, FSR 65 10.2 miles northwest.

FALLS CREEK HORSE CAMP (Gifford Pinchot National Forest)
5 units, trailers to 18', fishing, trailhead to Indian Heaven Wilderness.
Northwest of Carson. Cty 92135 9.0 miles northwest, FSR 6517 1.5 miles east, FSR 65 12.5 miles northeast.

LITTLE SODA SPRINGS (Gifford Pinchot National Forest)
4 units, no trailers, well, handpump, river, fishing.
Northwest of Carson. Cty 92135 13.6 miles northwest, FSR 5401 .9 miles south.

CHELAN

ANTILON LAKE (Wenatchee National Forest)
3 units, trailers to 18', lake – no motors, fishing.
Northwest of Chelan. State 150 5.8 miles northwest, Cty 10 5.2 miles north, FSR 3001 2.9 miles north.

BIG CREEK (Wenatchee National Forest)
3 tent units, stream, swimming, fishing, water skiing, near waterfall, boat-in only.
Northwest of Chelan. Boat 27.0 miles northwest.

CORRAL CREEK (Wenatchee National Forest)
2 tent units, lake, swimming, fishing, water skiing, boat in only.
Northwest of Chelan. Boat 27.6 miles northwest.

DEER POINT (Wenatchee National Forest)
6 tent units, lake, fishing, swimming, water skiing, boat-in only.
Northwest of Chelan. Boat 21.7 miles northwest.

DOMKE FALLS (Wenatchee National Forest)
4 units, lake, fishing, swimming, water skiing, boat-in only.
Northwest of Chelan. Boat 37.5 miles northwest.

DOMKE LAKE (Wenatchee National Forest)
6 tent units, lake, swimming, fishing, boat-in/hike-in or fly-in only.
Northwest of Chelan. Boat 40.0 miles northwest, Trail 1280 3.0 miles
south.

ELEPHANT ROCK (Wenatchee National Forest)
1 unit, lake, fishing, swimming, water skiing, boat-in only.
Northwest of Chelan. Boat 43.0 miles northwest.

GRAHAM HARBOR CREEK (Wenatchee National Forest)
11 units, stream, fishing, swimming, water skiing, boat-in only.
Northwest of Chelan. Boat 31.0 miles northwest.

GROUSE MOUNTAIN (Wenatchee National Forest)
4 tent units, piped water adjacent to Devil's Backbone ORV trails.
Northwest of Chelan. US 97 3.1 miles west, Cty 10 16.0 miles northwest,
FSR 298 8.1 miles west.

HANDY SPRING (Wenatchee National Forest)
1 unit, no trailers, piped water adjacent to Devil's Backbone ORV trails.
Northwest of Chelan. US 97 3.1 miles west, Cty 10 16.0 miles northwest,
FSR 298 14.5 miles west, FSR 298A .7 miles south.

HATCHERY (Wenatchee National Forest)
2 tent units, stream, swimming, fishing, boat-in/hike-in or fly-in only.
Northwest of Chelan. Boat 40.0 miles northwest, Trail 1280 3.0 miles
south, boat 1.0 mile southeast.

HOLDEN (Wenatchee National Forest)
2 tent units, stream, fishing, boat-in only, entry to Glacier Peak Wilderness.
Northwest of Chelan. Boat 41.2 miles northwest, FSR 3100 11.1 miles
west.

JUNIOR POINT (Wenatchee National Forest)
5 units, trailers to 18', no water, adjacent to Devil's Backbone ORV trail.
Northwest of Chelan. US 97 3.1 miles west, Cty 10 16 miles northwest,
FSR 298 14.3 miles west.

LUCERNE (Wenatchee National Forest)
2 tent units, well, lake, fishing, swimming, water skiing, Donke Lake trailhead, boat-in only.
Northwest of Chelan. Boat 41.2 miles northwest.

MITCHELL CREEK (Wenatchee National Forest)
11 tent units, stream, fishing, swimming, water skiing, boat-in only.
Northwest of Chelan. Boat 14.9 miles northwest.

PRINCE CREEK (Wenatchee National Forest)
5 units, stream, fishing, swimming, water skiing, boat-in only.
Northwest of Chelan. Boat 35.2 miles northwest.

REFRIGERATOR HARBOR (Wenatchee National Forest)
4 tent units, lake, Donke Lake trailhead, boat-in only.
Northwest of Chelan. Boat 41.0 miles northwest.

SAFETY HARBOR (Wenatchee National Forest)
2 tent units, fishing, swimming, water skiing, boat-in only.
Northwest of Chelan. Boat 25.0 miles northwest.

SOUTH NAVARRE (Wenatchee National Forest)
4 units, no trailers, piped water, horse camping, summit trail.
Northwest of Chelan. State 150 5.8 miles northwest, Cty 3010 5.2 miles
north, FSR 3001 36.5 miles northwest.

CHEWELAH

CHEWELAH (City)
Campsites, water, creek.
Follow signs to city park.

CLE ELUM

BEVERLY (Wenatchee National Forest)
16 units, trailers to 22', river, fishing, near hiking/motor cycle trails.
North of Cle Elum. US 970 8 miles east, Cty 107 13 miles north,
FSR 232 4 miles north.

BUCK MEADOWS (Wenatchee National Forest)
5 units, trailers to 18', stream, fishing.
South of Cle Elum. I-90 12 miles southeast, Cty 9123 3 miles south,
Cty 51 2 miles northwest, FSR 1902 6 miles northwest, FSR 1905
8 miles south, FSR 1807 5 miles south.

CLE ELUM RIVER (Wenatchee National Forest)
23 units, trailers to 22', river, fishing.
Northwest of Cle Elum. State 903 11.2 miles northwest, Cty 903 7 miles
northwest.

DE ROUX (Wenatchee National Forest)
4 tent units, stream, fishing, hiking, trail.
North of Cle Elum. US 97 8 miles east, FSR 107 13 miles north, FSR 232
8 miles northwest.

FISH LAKE (Wenatchee National Forest)
20 tent units, stream, fishing.
Northwest of Cle Elum. State 903 11.2 miles northwest, Cty 903 7 miles
northwest, FSR 2405 11.0 miles northeast.

OWHI (Wenatchee National Forest)
22 tent units, lake – no motors, boat launch, swimming, fishing, trailhead to
Alpine Lakes Wilderness.
Northwest of Cle Elum. State 903 11.2 miles northwest, Cty 903 9.7 miles
northwest, FSR 228 4.9 miles northwest, FSR 235 .2 miles north.

QUARTZ MOUNTAIN (Wenatchee National Forest)
3 units, trailers to 18', piped water, horse and ORV trails.
Southeast of Cle Elum. I-90 12.0 miles southeast, Cty 9123 3.0 miles
south, Cty 51 2.0 miles west, FSR 1902 6.0 miles northwest, FSR 1905
8 miles south, FSR 1904 4 miles west, FSR 1935 7 miles northwest.

RED MOUNTAIN (Wenatchee National Forest)
15 units, trailers to 18', river, fishing.
Northwest of Cle Elum. State 903 11.2 miles northwest, Cty 903 8.3 miles northwest.

SCATTER CREEK (Wenatchee National Forest)
12 units, trailers to 32', river, fishing.
Northwest of Cle Elum. State 903 11.2 miles northwest, Cty 903 11.0 miles northwest, FSR 2405 10.9 miles north.

SOUTH FORK MEADOW (Wenatchee National Forest)
4 units, trailers to 18', stream, fishing, hiking and motor cycle trails.
South of Cle Elum. I-90 12.0 miles southeast, Cty 9123 3.0 miles south, Cty 51 2.0 miles west, FSR 1902 11.0 miles northwest.

TAMARACK SPRING (Wenatchee National Forest)
2 tent units, piped water.
South of Cle Elum. I-90 12 miles southeast, Cty 9123 3.0 miles south, Cty 51 2.0 miles northwest, FSR 1902 6.0 miles northwest, FSR 1905 8.0 miles south, FSR 1904 2.0 miles east.

TUCQUALA MEADOWS (Wenatchee National Forest)
9 units, trailers to 18', stream, trailhead to Alpine Lakes Wilderness.
Northwest of Cle Elum. State 903 11.2 miles northwest, Cty 903 10.7 miles northwest, FSR 2405 12.9 miles northeast.

COLVILLE

TWIN LAKES (Colville National Forest)
16 units, trailers to 18', well, boat launch, fishing.
East of Colville. State 294 12.5 miles east, Cty 633 1.5 miles north, FSR 617 4.5 miles north.

CONCONULLY

KERR (Okanogan National Forest)
9 units, trailers to 22', stream, fishing.
Northwest of Conconully. Cty 2361 1.8 miles northwest, FSR 38 2.0 miles northwest.

SUGARLOAF (Okanogan National Forest)
5 units, trailers to 22', well, lake, boat launch, swimming, fishing.
Northeast of Conconully. Cty 4015 4.5 miles northwest.

TIFFANY SPRING (Okanogan National Forest)
3 units.
Northwest of Conconully. Cty 2017 1.8 miles southwest, FSR 37 21.2 miles northwest, FSR 39 7.5 miles northeast.

CONCRETE

BOULDER CREEK (Mt. Baker-Snoqualmie National Forest)
10 units, trailers to 18', stream.
North of Concrete. Cty 25 9.6 miles north, FSR 11 5.4 miles north.

MAPLE GROVE (Mt. Baker-Snoqualmie National Forest)
6 tent units, boat-in or hike-in only, swimming, fishing, water skiing, trails.
North of Concrete. Cty 25 9.6 miles north, FSR 11 2.4 miles north,
FSR 1118 2 miles east, boat or hike 1.6 miles north along east shore of
Baker Lake.

PARK CREEK (Mt. Baker-Snoqualmie National Forest)
12 units, trailers to 18', stream.
North of Concrete. Cty 25 9.6 miles north, FSR 11 7.4 miles north,
FSR 1144 .1 mile northwest.

SHANNON CREEK (Mt. Baker-Snoqualmie National Forest)
20 units, trailers to 22', lake, boat launch, swimming, fishing, water skiing.
Northeast of Concrete. Cty FH25 9.6 miles north, FSR 11 12.2 miles
north, FSR 3830 .5 miles southeast.

CURLEW

DEER CREEK SUMMIT (Colville National Forest)
4 units, trailers to 18', hiking trails.
East of Curlew. Cty 602 11.5 miles east.

COUGAR

LOWER FALLS (Gifford Pinchot National Forest)
25 units, trailers to 18', on Lewis River, fishing, hiking, trails, waterfalls.
East of Cougar. FSR 90 15 miles east to Pine Creek Information Station,
FSR 90 13 miles east.

DARRINGTON

DOWNEY CREEK (Mt. Baker-Snoqualmie National Forest)
5 tent units, stream, fishing, Glacier Peak Wilderness.
East of Darrington. Cty road 7.7 miles north, FSR 26 20.8 miles southeast.

FRENCH CREEK (Mt. Baker-Snoqualmie National Forest)
3 units, trailers to 22', stream.
West of Darrington. State 530 8.1 miles west, FSR 2010 .8 miles south.

DAYTON

GODMAN (Umatilla National Forest)
7 units, trailers to 18', piped water.
Southeast of Dayton. Cty 118 14.8 miles southeast, FSR 46 11.0 miles
south.

TEEPEE (Umatilla National Forest)
7 units, trailers to 18'.
Southeast of Dayton. Cty 118 14.8 miles southeast, FSR 46 11.0 miles
south, FSR 4608 5.0 miles northeast.

ELBE

ALDER LAKE (Dept. of Natural Resources)
25 campsites, drinking water, boat launch, fishing.
West of Elbe. Hwy 7 south to Pleasant Valley Road. Keep left at the
Y and follow to campground.

ELBE HILLS ORV TRAILHEAD (Dept. of Natural Resources)
5 campsites, no water, jeep trails.
East of Elbe. Take Hwy 706 east and turn left just before National.
This will lead to the campground.

ELLENSBURG

ESMERELDA (Wenatchee National Forest)
3 units, trailers to 18', stream, fishing, horse trails.
South of Ellensburg. US 97 8 miles east, Cty 107 13 miles north, FSR 232
9 miles northwest.

LION ROCK SPRING (Wenatchee National Forest)
3 tent units, piped water, hiking trails, horse and cycle trails nearby.
North of Ellensburg. Cty 179 12.4 miles north, FSR 2008 9.7 miles north,
FSR 2008E .8 miles west.

ENTIAT

FOX CREEK (Wenatchee National Forest)
9 units, trailers to 18', river, fishing.
Northwest of Entiat. US 97 1.4 miles southwest, Cty 371 25.2 miles
northwest, FSR 317 1.8 miles northwest.

LAKE CREEK (Wenatchee National Forest)
11 units, trailers to 18', fishing.
Northwest of Entiat. US 97 1.4 miles southwest, Cty 371 25.2 miles
northwest, FSR 317 3.0 miles northwest.

NORTH FORK (Wenatchee National Forest)
7 tent units, 1 trailer to 22', river, fishing.
Northwest of Entiat. US 97 1.4 miles southwest, Cty 371 25.2 miles
northwest, FSR 317 8.3 miles northwest.

PINE FLAT (Wenatchee National Forest)
8 tent units, 1 trailer to 22', river, fishing.
Northwest of Entiat. US 97 1.4 miles southwest, Cty 371 10 miles
northwest, FSR 2710 3.7 miles northwest.

SPRUCE GROVE (Wenatchee National Forest)
2 tent units, river, fishing.
Northwest of Entiat. US 97 1.4 miles southwest, Cty 371 25.2 miles
northwest, FSR 317 9.8 miles northwest.

THREE CREEK (Wenatchee National Forest)
3 tent units, river, fishing.
Northwest of Entiat. US 97 1.4 miles southwest, Cty 371 25.2 miles
northwest, FSR 317 10.5 miles northwest.

ENUMCLAW

BUCK CREEK (Mt. Baker-Snoqualmie National Forest)
20 tent units, 50 unit trailer parking, horse trails, hiking, berry picking.
Southeast of Enumclaw. State 410 36 miles southeast, FSR 7160
1 mile to campground.

CORRAL PASS (Mt. Baker-Snoqualmie National Forest)
12 tent units, no trailers, stream, near Mountain Goat Reserve and Norse Peak Wilderness.
Southeast of Enumclaw. US 410 31.0 miles southeast, FSR 7174 6.1 miles east.

EVANS CREEK O. R. V. CAMP (Mt. Baker-Snoqualmie National Forest)
26 tent/trailer units, stream.
South of Enumclaw. Located on the south side of Mt. Rainier, 35 miles south of Enumclaw on State 165, FSR 7920 at junction.

GOVERNMENT MEADOW (Mt. Baker-Snoqualmie National Forest)
2 tent units, stream, hike-in only, on Pacific Crest Trail.
Southeast of Enumclaw. US 410 18.7 miles southeast, FSR 70 8.1 miles east, Trail 1175 6.3 miles southeast.

TWIN CAMP (Mt. Baker-Snoqualmie National Forest)
3 tent units, no trailers, spring, volunteer maintenance only.
Southeast of Enumclaw. US 410 20.0 miles east, FSR 70 7.3 miles east, FSR 7030 3 miles northeast.

FORKS

COTTONWOOD (Dept. of Natural Resources)
6 campsites, river, drinking water.
Southeast of Forks. Take US 101 approximately 14 miles south to Cty Rd. and turn right. Campground road is on left 2.3 miles.

HOH OXBOW (Dept. of Natural Resources)
Campsites, river.
Southeast of Forks. Take US 101 approximately 14 miles south to campground.

MINNIE PETERSON (Dept. of Natural Resources)
6 campsites, river, drinking water.
Southeast of Forks. Take US 101 approximately 13 miles south to Valley Rd. Campground is 4.5 miles.

SOUTH FORK HOH (Dept. of Natural Resources)
3 campsites, river.
Southeast of Forks. Take US 101 approximately 15 miles south to Hoh Mainline Rd. After 7 miles turn left for 1.2 miles, then left again. Take the first right, another left and follow 5.9 miles to campground.

WILLOUGHBY CREEK (Dept. of Natural Resources)
3 campsites, river.
Southeast of Forks. Take US 101 approximately 13 miles south to Valley Rd. Campground is 3 miles.

GLACIER

CANYON CREEK (Mt. Baker-Snoqualmie National Forest)
6 units, trailers to 18', stream, fishing.
North of Glacier. State 542 2 miles northeast, FSR 31 7.1 miles north.

BEAVER PLANT LAKE (Dept. of Natural Resources)
Campsites, hike-in only.
Southeast of Granite Falls. Take Cty Road FH7 approximately 15 miles
to FSR 3015. Follow this road another 4 miles, staying left at the T to
parking lot. Campground is 1 mile along trail.

BEDAL (Mt. Baker-Snoqualmie National Forest)
18 units, trailers to 22', river, fishing.
East of Granite Falls. Cty FH7 30.1 miles east, FSR 20 6.5 miles
northeast.

BOARDMAN LAKE (Mt. Baker-Snoqualmie National Forest)
8 tent units, lake – no motors, swimming, fishing, trails, hike-in only.
Southeast of Granite Falls. Cty FH7 15.5 miles east, FSR 4020 6.9 miles
south, Trail 704 1 mile south.

DICK SPERRY (Mt. Baker-Snoqualmie National Forest)
4 units, trailers to 18', river, fishing.
East of Granite Falls. Cty FH7 20.8 miles.

GOAT LAKE (Mt. Baker-Snoqualmie National Forest)
10 tent units, lake, swimming, fishing, trails, hike-in only.
East of Granite Falls. Cty FH7 30.1 miles east, FSR 20 3.4 miles
northeast, FSR 4080 .7 miles southeast, Trail 647 4.5 miles southeast.

LOWER ASHLAND LAKE (Dept. of Natural Resources)
Campsites, hike-in only.
Southeast of Granite Falls. Take Cty FH7 approximately 15 miles to
FSR 3015. Follow this road another 4 miles, staying left at the T to
parking lot. Campground is 2 miles along trail.

MONTE CRISTO (Mt. Baker-Snoqualmie National Forest)
5 tent units, stream.
Southeast of Granite Falls. Cty FH7 30.1 miles east, Cty MC 4.1 miles
southeast.

PERRY CREEK (Mt. Baker-Snoqualmie National Forest)
8 units, trailers to 18', stream, fishing.
East of Granite Falls. Cty FH7 25.8 miles east.

RED BRIDGE (Mt. Baker-Snoqualmie National Forest)
16 units, trailers to 32', river, fishing.
East of Granite Falls. Cty FH7 18.1 miles east.

RIVER BAR (Mt. Baker-Snoqualmie National Forest)
15 units, trailers to 32', river, fishing.
East of Granite Falls. Cty FH7 18.6 miles east.

TWIN FALLS LAKE (Dept. of Natural Resources)
Campsites, hike-in only.
Southeast of Granite Falls. Take Cty FH7 approximately 15 miles to
FSR 3015. Follow this road another 4 miles, staying left at the T to
parking lot. Campground is 3 miles along trail.

UPPER ASHLAND LAKE (Dept. of Natural Resources)
Campsites, hike-in only.
Southeast of Granite Falls. Take Cty FH7 approximately 15 miles to
FSR 3015. Follow this road another 4 miles staying left at the T to
parking lot. Campground is 1.5 miles along trail.

HOODSPORT

BIG CREEK (Olympic National Forest)
23 units, trailers to 22', swimming, fishing, hiking trail.
West of Hoodsport. Cty 9420 8.0 miles west, FSR 24 .1 mile south.

HUNTERS

CLOVER LEAF (Coulee Dam Recreation Area)
8 units, boat dock, water.
North of Hunters and just south of Gifford on Hwy. 25.

DETILLON (Coulee Dam Recreation Area)
12 campsites, boat-in only, water.
South of Hunters along Hwy 20 to its junction with the Spokane River.
East approximately 8 miles upriver.

ENTERPRISE (Coulee Dam Recreation Area)
4 campsites, boat-in only.
Southwest of Hunters approximately 8 miles, on the east bank of FDR Lake.

HAWK CREEK (Coulee Dam Recreation Area)
16 units, trailers okay, water, boat ramp.
Take Hwy 25 south of Hunters to Fort Spokane. Campground is approximately 6 miles southwest along the road to Creston.

JONES BAY (Coulee Dam Recreation Area)
2 campsites, boat-in only.
Southwest of Hunters. Approximately 6 miles east of the San Poil
River's junction with FDR Lake on the lake's shore.

INDEX

TROUBLESOME CREEK (Mt. Baker-Snoqualmie National Forest)
16 units, trailers to 22', river, fishing, trails.
Northeast of Index. Cty 290 12.0 miles northeast.

IONE

EDGEWATER (Colville National Forest)
23 units, trailers to 22', piped water, river, boat launch, fishing, water skiing.
Northwest of Ione. State 31 1.0 mile south, Cty 303 .3 miles east,
Cty 306 2.0 miles north, FSR 1724 1.8 miles north.

WEST BRANCH LECLERC CREEK (Colville National Forest)
8 units, trailers to 22', fishing.
Southeast of Ione. Cty 2 6.0 miles east, FSR 307 10.0 miles southeast.

KETTLE FALLS

BRADBURY (Coulee Dam Recreation Area)
5 units, boat ramp.
South of Kettle Falls via Hwy 25 approximately 8 miles.

CANYON CREEK (Colville National Forest)
12 units, trailers to 32', well, fishing.
West of Kettle Falls. US 395 3.5 miles northwest, State 20 11.0 miles west, FSR 2000 .2 miles south.

HAAG COVE (Coulee Dam Recreation Area)
12 units, trailers okay, water.
Southwest of Kettle Falls. Cross the river on Hwy 20 and follow the west bank of FDR Lake to the campground.

KAMLOOPS ISLAND (Coulee Dam Recreation Area)
7 campsites.
Northwest of Kettle Falls. Take Hwy 20 west across the river and follow US 395 north approximately 4 miles to campground.

KETTLE RIVER (Coulee Dam Recreation Area)
4 units, boat-in only.
Northwest of Kettle Falls. Up the Kettle River just below Boyd.

MARCUS ISLAND (Coulee Dam Recreation Area)
7 campsites.
North of Kettle Falls approximately 5 miles via Hwy 25.

NE LAKE ELLEN (Colville National Forest)
11 units, trailers to 22', well, boat launch, fishing.
Southwest of Kettle Falls. US 395 3.5 miles northwest, State 20 4.0 miles south, Cty 2014 4.5 miles southwest, FSR 2014 5.5 miles southwest.

NORTH GORGE (Coulee Dam Recreation Area)
9 units, trailers okay, water, boat ramp, on Columbia River.
North of Kettle Falls. Hwy 25 approximately 18 miles north of Kettle Falls.

SHERMAN CREEK (Coulee Dam Recreation Area)
5 campsites, boat-in only.
Southwest of Kettle Falls. Take Hwy 20 approximately 6 miles to campground.

SNAG COVE (Coulee Dam Recreation Area)
3 units, trailers okay, water, on west bank of Columbia River.
Northwest of Kettle Falls. Hwy 20 west across river, US 395 north 4 miles, right 8 miles to campground.

TROUT LAKE (Colville National Forest)
4 units, trailers to 18', piped water, boat launch, fishing.
West of Kettle Falls. US 395 3.5 miles northwest, State 20 5.5 miles west, FSR 2000 5.0 miles northwest.

ALDER CREEK (Wenatchee National Forest)
Campsites.
Northwest of Leavenworth. US 2 .3 miles east, State 209 18.3 miles north, FSR 2746 4.5 miles west.

ALPINE MEADOW (Wenatchee National Forest)
4 tent units, no trailers, river, fishing.
Northwest of Leavenworth. US 2 15.9 miles northwest, State 207 4.0 miles north, Cty 22 1.0 mile east, FSR 311 19.5 miles northwest.

ATKINSON (Wenatchee National Forest)
8 units, trailers to 22', river, fishing.
Northwest of Leavenworth. US 2 15.9 miles northwest, State 207 4.0 miles north, Cty 22 1.0 mile east, FSR 311 15.0 miles northwest.

BLACKPINE CREEK HORSECAMP (Wenatchee National Forest)
5 units, trailers to 22', fishing, horse trails.
West of Leavenworth. US 2 .5 miles southeast, Cty 71 2.9 miles south, FSR 2451 15.0 miles northwest.

BLUE POOL (Wenatchee National Forest)
2 units, trailers to 18', river, fishing.
North of Leavenworth. US 2 15.0 miles northwest, State 207 4.0 miles north, Cty 22 1.2 miles northeast, FSR 311 16.0 miles north.

DEER CAMP (Wenatchee National Forest)
3 tent units, no trailers.
Northeast of Leavenworth. US 2 .3 miles east, State 209 14.5 miles north, Cty 22 3.0 miles northeast, FSR 2746 1.5 miles north, FSR 2722 2.0 miles northeast.

DEEP CREEK (Wenatchee National Forest)
3 units.
North of Leavenworth. US 2 .3 miles east, State 209 17.5 miles north, FSR 2476 2.2 miles north.

FINNER (Wenatchee National Forest)
3 tent units, some trailers, stream, fishing, trails.
Northwest of Leavenworth. US 2 15.9 miles northwest, State 207 4.0 miles north, Cty 22 1.0 mile east, FSR 311 11.0 miles northwest.

FISH POND (Wenatchee National Forest)
3 tent units, stream, fishing, no trailers.
Northwest of Leavenworth. US 2 15.9 miles northwest, State 207 .8 miles northeast.

GOOSE CREEK (Wenatchee National Forest)
5 units, some trailers.
North of Leavenworth. US 2 .3 miles east, State 209 17.5 miles north, FSR 2746 3.2 miles north.

GRASSHOPPER MEADOWS (Wenatchee National Forest)
4 tent units, river, fishing.
Northwest of Leavenworth. US 2 15.9 miles northwest, State 207 8.4 miles north, Cty 22 .9 miles northwest, FSR 293 7.9 miles northwest.

IDA CREEK (Wenatchee National Forest)
4 units, trailers to 22', fishing.
West of Leavenworth. US 2 .5 miles southwest, Cty 71 2.9 miles south, FSR 2451 10.2 miles northwest.

LAKE CREEK (Wenatchee National Forest)
8 tent units, stream, fishing, trailers to 32'.
Northwest of Leavenworth. US 2 15.9 miles northwest, State 207 8.4 miles north, Cty 22 1.5 miles west, FSR 283 9.8 miles west.

LITTLE WENATCHEE FORD (Wenatchee National Forest)
3 tent units, stream, fishing, no trailers.
Northwest of Leavenworth. US 2 15.9 miles northwest, State 207 8.4 miles north, Cty 22 1.5 miles west, FSR 283 14.7 miles northwest.

MEADOW CREEK (Wenatchee National Forest)
4 units, no trailers, fishing.
North of Leavenworth. US 2 15.9 miles northwest, State 207 4.0 miles northeast, Cty 22 1.0 mile east, FSR 311 2.4 miles northeast, FSR 2815 2.1 miles northwest.

NAPEEQUA (Wenatchee National Forest)
5 units, some trailers to 32', river, fishing, Glacier Peak Wilderness entrance.
Northwest of Leavenworth. US 2 15.9 miles northwest, State 207 8.4 miles north, Cty 22 .9 miles northwest, FSR 293 5.9 miles northwest.

NINETEEN MILE (Wenatchee National Forest)
3 units, trailers to 22', river, fishing.
Northwest of Leavenworth. US 2 15.9 miles northwest, State 207 4.0 miles north, Cty 22 1.0 mile east, FSR 311 18.0 miles northwest.

PHELPS CREEK (Wenatchee National Forest)
7 units, no trailers, fishing, horse trails to Glacier Peak Wilderness.
Northwest of Leavenworth. US 2 15.9 miles northwest, State 207 4.0 miles north, Cty 22 1.0 mile east, FSR 311 21.0 miles northwest.

RIVERSIDE (Wenatchee National Forest)
6 tent units, river, fishing, trailers to 32'.
Northwest of Leavenworth. US 2 15.9 miles northwest, State 207 8.4 miles north, Cty 22 1.5 miles west, FSR 283 5.9 miles west.

ROCK CREEK (Wenatchee National Forest)
4 units, trailers to 22', fishing, trails.
Northwest of Leavenworth. US 2 15.9 miles northwest, State 207 4.0 miles north, Cty 22 1.0 mile east, FSR 311 13.0 miles northwest.

ROCK ISLAND (Wenatchee National Forest)
18 units, trailers to 22', stream, fishing.
West of Leavenworth. US 2 .5 miles southwest, Cty 71 2.9 miles south, FSR 2451 13.7 miles northwest.

SCHAEFER CREEK (Wenatchee National Forest)
5 units, fishing.
Northwest of Leavenworth. US 2 15.9 miles northwest, State 207 4.0 miles north, Cty 22 1.0 mile east, FSR 311 14.0 miles northwest.

SODA SPRINGS (Wenatchee National Forest)
5 tent units, stream, fishing, trails, no trailers.
Northwest of Leavenworth.   US 2   15.9 miles northwest, State 207
8.4 miles north, Cty 22 1.5 miles west, FSR 283 7.2 miles west.

THESEUS CREEK (Wenatchee National Forest)
2 units, trailers to 18', fishing.
Northwest of Leavenworth.   US 2   15.9 miles northwest, State 207
9.0 miles northwest, FSR 283 6.0 miles west, FSR 2713 4.5 miles west.

WHITE RIVER FALLS (Wenatchee National Forest)
5 tent units, river, fishing, no trailers, Glacier Peak Wilderness entrance.
Northwest of Leavenworth.   US 2   15.9 miles northwest, State 207
8.4 miles north, Cty 22 .9 miles northwest. FSR 293 9.0 miles northwest.

LOOMIS

CHOPAKA LAKE (Dept. of Natural Resources)
15 units, boat launch, water, fishing.
Northwest of Loomis.   Palmer Lake road north, Chopaka Creek road
northwest to campground.

COLD SPRINGS (Dept. of Natural Resources)
9 campsites in mountainous area, spring water.
Northwest of Loomis.   Palmer Lake road north, Chopaka Creek road
northwest, campground is at the end of the road.

FOURTEEN MILE (Okanogan National Forest)
8 units, trailers to 18', stream, fishing, hiking trails.
Northwest of Loomis. Cty 9425 2.1 miles northwest, FSR 39 8.1 miles
southwest, Road T1100 4.6 miles northwest.

LONG SWAMP (Okanogan National Forest)
2 units, trailers to 18'.
West of Loomis. Cty 9425 2.1 miles north, Cty 4066 1.0 mile north,
FSR 39 20.5 miles west.

NORTH FORK NINE MILE (Dept. of Natural Resources)
11 units, water, hiking trails, fishing.
Northwest of Loomis.   Palmer Lake road north, Chopaka Creek road
northwest, Nine Mile Creek road south to campground.

TOATS JUNCTION (Dept. of Natural Resources)
9 units, hiking trails.
Northwest of Loomis.   Palmer Lake road north, Chopaka Creek road
west, Coulee Creek road northwest to campground.

MARBLEMOUNT

MARBLE CREEK (Mt. Baker-Snoqualmie National Forest)
20 units, trailers to 18', river, fishing.
East of Marblemount. Cty 3528 8.0 miles east, FSR 1530 1.0 mile south.

METALINE FALLS

CRESCENT LAKE (Colville National Forest)
13 units, trailers to 32', fishing.
North of Metaline Falls. State 31 11.0 miles north.

NACHES

BUMPING CROSS (Wenatchee National Forest)
12 units, trailers to 18', river, fishing, reduced service.
Northwest of Naches. US 12 4.3 miles west, State 410 27.8 miles northwest.

BUMPING DAM (Wenatchee National Forest)
28 units, trailers to 18', river, fishing, reduced service, adjacent boat launch.
Northwest of Naches. US 12 4.3 miles west, State 410 27.8 miles northwest, FSR 174 10.8 miles southwest, FSR 1602 .6 miles north.

CLEAR LAKE NORTH (Wenatchee National Forest)
35 units, lake, stream, fishing, hiking, boating – 5 mph speed limit.
West of Naches. US 12 35.6 miles west, FSR 143 9 miles south, FSR 1312 .5 miles south.

CLEAR LAKE SOUTH (Wenatchee National Forest)
26 units, stream, lake– 5 mph speed limit, fishing, hiking, boating, drinking water.
West of Naches. US 12 35.6 miles west, FSR 143 .9 miles south, FSR 1312 1 mile south.

CROW CREEK (Wenatchee National Forest)
15 units, trailers to 18', fishing, ORV, reduced service.
Northwest of Naches. US 12 4.3 miles west, State 410 24.5 miles northwest, FSR 197 2.7 miles northwest, FSR 182 .4 miles west.

HALFWAY FLAT (Wenatchee National Forest)
12 units, river, fishing, reduced service.
Northwest of Naches. US 12 4.3 miles west, State 410 21.0 miles northwest, FSR 175 2.9 miles northwest.

MILK POND (Wenatchee National Forest)
5 units, lake, fishing, hiking.
West of Naches. US 12 4.3 miles west, State 410 25 miles northwest, FSR 173 northeast 1.7 miles.

PENINSULA (Wenatchee National Forest)
19 units, trailers to 18', lake, swimming, fishing, water skiing, boat launch.
Southwest of Naches. US 12 23.0 miles west, FSR 143 2.9 miles south, FSR 1382 1.5 miles west.

PINE NEEDLE (Wenatchee National Forest)
6 units, no trailers, river, fishing, reduced service.
Northwest of Naches. US 12 4.3 miles west, State 410 30.1 miles northwest.

PLEASANT VALLEY (Wenatchee National Forest)
18 units, trailers to 22', river, fishing, reduced service.
Northwest of Naches. US 12 4.3 miles west, State 410 36.1 miles northwest.

RIMROCK PUBLIC BOAT LANDING (Wenatchee National Forest)
5 units, lake, fishing, swimming, boating, water skiing.
West of Naches. US 12 29.6 miles to campground.

SODA SPRINGS (Wenatchee National Forest)
19 units, stream, fishing, hiking, mineral water.
West of Naches. US 12 4.3 miles west, State 410 28.6 miles northwest, FSR 174 5 miles southwest.

SOUTH FORK (Wenatchee National Forest)
9 units, trailers to 18', river, fishing, reduced service.
Southwest of Naches. US 12 23.0 miles west, FSR 143 4.0 miles south, FSR 1326 .5 miles south.

WILD ROSE (Wenatchee National Forest)
8 units, trailers to 32', river, fishing, reduced service.
West of Naches. US 12 20.9 miles west.

NORTH BEND

COMMONWEALTH (Mt. Baker-Snoqualmie National Forest)
6 units, no trailers, stream, close to Pacific Crest National Scenic Trail.
Southeast of North Bend at Snoqualmie Pass. I-90 22.6 miles southeast, FSR 58 .2 miles north.

TAYLOR RIVER (Mt. Baker-Snoqualmie National Forest)
20 tent units, no trailers, river, fishing.
Northeast of Bend. I-90 3.9 miles southeast, FSR 56 14.8 miles northeast, FSR 5620 1.3 miles southeast, FSR 5130 .5 miles west.

OKANOGAN

LEADER LAKE (Dept. of Natural Resources)
16 units, boat launch, fishing.
West of Okanogan via Hwy 20 to Leader Lake Road.

ROCK CREEK (Dept. of Natural Resources)
6 units, water, hiking trails.
Northwest of Okanogan. Hwy 20 west, Loup Loup Creek Road north to campground.

ROCK LAKES (Dept. of Natural Resources)
8 units, hiking trails, fishing.
Northwest of Okanogan. Hwy 20 west, Loup Loup Creek Road north, Rock Lakes Road northwest to campground.

ORIENT

PIERRE LAKE (Colville National Forest)
15 units, trailers to 32', well, boat launch, swimming, fishing, water skiing.
Northeast to Orient. Cty 15101 3.8 miles east, Cty 1500 3.2 miles north.

SUMMIT LAKE (Colville National Forest)
5 units, no trailers, well, boat launch, fishing.
Northeast of Orient. Cty 1510 3.8 miles east, Cty 1500 5.0 miles north,
FSR 1500 3.0 miles north.

PACKWOOD

DOG LAKE (Wenatchee National Forest)
11 units, trailers to 18', boat launch, fishing, hiking trails, reduced service.
Northeast of Packwood. US 12 22.2 miles northeast.

HATCHERY RV CAMP (Gifford Pinchot National Forest)
23 units, trailers to 22', river, fishing, near Mt. Rainier National Park.
Northeast of Packwood. US 12 2.1 miles northeast, FSR 1272 .8 miles
west.

SODA SPRINGS (Gifford Pinchot National Forest)
9 tent units, no trailers, fishing, trailhead to William O. Douglas Wilderness.
Northeast of Packwood. US 12 8.5 miles northeast, FSR 4510 5.5 miles
west.

SUMMIT CREEK (Gifford Pinchot National Forest)
7 tent units, no trailers, fishing.
Northeast of Packwood. US 12 8.9 miles northeast, FSR 4510 2.1 miles
north.

WALUPT LAKE (Gifford Pinchot National Forest)
35 units, trailers to 18', no water, fishing, hiking trails, boat launch, trailhead to Goat Rocks Wilderness.
Southeast of Packwood. US 12 2.7 miles southwest, FSR 21 16.4 miles
southeast, FSR 2160 4.5 miles east.

WALUPT LAKE HORSE CAMP (Gifford Pinchot National Forest)
6 units, trailers to 18', fishing, horse trails, trailhead to Goat Rocks
Wilderness.
Southeast of Packwood. US 12 2.7 miles southwest, FSR 21 16.4 miles
southeast, FSR 2160 3.5 miles east.

WHITE PASS LAKE (Wenatchee National Forest)
12 units, trailers to 18', lake – no motors, boat launch, swimming, fishing,
reduced service.
Northeast of Packwood. US 12 20.9 miles northeast, FSR 1310 .3 miles
north.

WHITE PASS HORSE CAMP (Wenatchee National Forest)
5 units, lake, fishing, hiking trails, reduced service.
Northeast of Packwood. US 12 19.0 miles northeast.

POMEROY

ALDER THICKET (Umatilla National Forest)
6 units, trailers to 18'.
South of Pomeroy. State 128 9.1 miles south, Cty 107 7.7 miles south,
FSR 40 3.3 miles south.

BIG SPRINGS (Umatilla National Forest)
6 units, trailers to 18', piped water.
Southeast of Pomeroy. State 128 14.8 miles southeast, Cty 191 3.4 miles south, FSR 42000 5.1 miles southwest.

FOREST BOUNDARY (Umatilla National Forest)
5 units, trailers to 32'.
South of Pomeroy. State 128 9.1 miles south, Cty 107 7.7 miles south, FSR 40 .1 mile south.

MISERY SPRINGS (Umatilla National Forest)
5 units, trailers to 18'.
Southeast of Pomeroy. State 128 9.1 miles south, Cty 107 7.7 miles southeast, FSR 40 16.2 miles southeast, FSR 4030 .5 miles south.

PANJAB (Umatilla National Forest)
6 units, trailers to 18', river.
Southwest of Pomeroy. Cty 101 17.6 miles southwest, FSR 47 12.1 miles southwest, FSR 4713 .2 miles south.

PATAHA (Umatilla National Forest)
7 units, trailers to 18', stream.
Southeast of Pomeroy. State 128 10.6 miles south, Cty 185 5.0 miles south, FSR 4016 .3 miles south, FSR 20 1.3 miles west.

SPRUCE SPRING (Umatilla National Forest)
4 units, trailers to 18', piped water.
South of Pomeroy. State 128 9.1 miles south, Cty 107 7.7 miles south, FSR 40 10.9 miles southeast.

TEAL SPRING (Umatilla National Forest)
8 units, trailers to 18', piped water.
South of Pomeroy. State 128 9.1 miles south, Cty 107 7.7 miles south, FSR 40 8.8 miles south, FSR 200 .3 miles south.

TUCANNON (Umatilla National Forest)
15 units, trailers to 18', piped water.
Southwest of Pomeroy. Cty 101 17.0 miles southwest, FSR 47 8.1 miles southwest, FSR 160 .2 miles south.

QUEETS

COPPERMINE BOTTOM (Dept. of Natural Resources)
9 campsites, river.
Northeast of Queets. Take US 101 southeast 5.4 miles to Clearwater road. After approximately 7.5 miles turn right and follow road 3-4 miles to campground.

UPPER CLEARWATER (Dept. of Natural Resources)
6 campsites, river.
Northeast of Queets. Take US 101 southeast 5.4 miles to the Clearwater road. After approximately 12.5 miles turn right and follow road 3-4 miles to campground.

ADAMS FORK (Gifford Pinchot National Forest)
23 units, trailers to 22', hand pump, well, on Cispus River, fishing, hiking trails.
Southeast of Randle. Cty Road 3.1 miles south, FSR 23 15.7 miles southeast, FSR 21 4.7 miles southeast, FSR 5601 .2 miles east.

BLUE LAKE CREEK (Gifford Pinchot National Forest)
11 units, trailers to 22', water, on Cispus River, fishing, hiking trails.
Southeast of Randle. Cty Road 3.1 miles south, FSR 23 13.2 miles southeast.

CAT CREEK (Gifford Pinchot National Forest)
6 units, trailers to 22', on Cispus River, fishing, hiking trails.
Southeast of Randle. Cty Road 3.1 miles south, FSR 23 15.7 miles southeast, FSR 21 6.1 miles east.

CHAIN-OF-LAKES (Gifford Pinchot National Forest)
3 units, trailers to 18', lake – no motors, swimming, fishing, hiking trails, near Mt. Adams Wilderness.
Southeast of Randle. Cty Road 3.1 miles south, FSR 23 28.9 miles southeast, FSR 2329 1.2 miles north, FSR 22 1.0 mile north.

COUNCIL LAKE (Gifford Pinchot National Forest)
11 units, trailers to 22', boat launch, swimming, fishing, hiking trails, near Mt. Adams Wilderness.
Southeast of Randle. Cty Road 3.1 miles south, FSR 23 30.2 miles southeast, FSR 2334 1.2 miles west.

HORSESHOE LAKE (Gifford Pinchot National Forest)
10 units, trailers to 18', boat launch, swimming, fishing, hiking trails, near Mt. Adams Wilderness.
Southeast of Randle. Cty Road 3.1 miles south, FSR 23 28.9 miles southeast, FSR 2329 6.8 miles northeast, FSR 78 1.3 miles west.

KEENES HORSE CAMP (Gifford Pinchot National Forest)
15 units, trailers to 22', stream, swimming, fishing, horse trails, hiking trails, near Mt. Adams Wilderness.
Southeast of Randle. Cty Road 3.1 miles southeast, FSR 23 28.9 miles southeast, FSR 2329 7.2 miles southeast.

KILLEN CREEK (Gifford Pinchot National Forest)
8 units, trailers to 18', fishing, trailhead to Mt. Adams Wilderness.
Southeast of Randle. Cty Road 3.1 miles south, FSR 23 28.9 miles southeast, FSR 2329 6.2 miles southeast, FSR 72 .1 mile west.

OLALLIE LAKE (Gifford Pinchot National Forest)
6 units, trailers to 18', lake, boat launch, swimming, fishing, hiking trails.
Southeast of Randle. Cty Road 3.1 miles south, FSR 23 28.9 miles southeast, FSR 2329 .8 miles north, FSR 5601 .6 miles north.

POLE PATCH (Gifford Pinchot National Forest)
13 units, trailers to 22', stream, berry picking.
South of Randle. Cty Road 2.0 miles south, FSR 25 20.3 miles south, FSR 28 2.8 miles east, FSR 77 6.1 miles north.

SPRING CREEK (Gifford Pinchot National Forest)
3 units, trailers to 18', fishing, hiking trails, near Mt. Adams Wilderness.
Southeast of Randle. Cty Road 3.1 miles south, FSR 23 28.9 miles southeast, FSR 2329 7.5 miles northeast.

TAKHLAKH (Gifford Pinchot National Forest)
54 units, trailers to 22', no water, lake, boat launch, swimming, fishing, hiking trails.
Southeast of Randle. Cty Road 3.1 miles south, FSR 23 28.9 miles southeast, FSR 2329 1.6 miles north.

REPUBLIC

KETTLE RANGE (Colville National Forest)
9 units, trailers to 22', well, hiking trails.
East of Republic. State 21 .5 miles east, State 30 18.0 miles east.

TEN MILE (Colville National Forest)
9 units, trailers to 18', piped water, fishing.
South of Republic. State 21 10.0 miles south.

RIVERSIDE

CRAWFISH LAKE (Okanogan National Forest)
22 units, trailers to 32', boat launch, fishing, water skiing.
East of Riverside. Cty 9320 17.7 miles east, FSR 30 2.1 miles south.

SAN JUAN ISLANDS

CYPRESS HEAD (Dept. of Natural Resources)
5 units, boat-in only, mooring buoys.
In San Juan Islands.

JAMES ISLAND (Washington State)
Campsites, boat-in only, picnic facilities, hiking trails.
In San Juan Islands.

JONES ISLAND (Washington State)
Campsites, boat-in only, picnic facilities, hiking.
In San Juan Islands.

LONG ISLAND (Washington State)
5 campgrounds, tables, boat-in only.
In San Juan Islands.

SKAGIT ISLAND (Washington State)
Campsites, boat-in only, mooring buoys.
In San Juan Islands.

SEQUIM

DUNGENESS FORKS (Olympic National Forest)
9 tent units, no trailers, well, river, fishing, hiking trails.
South of Sequim. US 101 4.0 miles southeast, Cty 9537 4.5 miles south, FSR 2958 3.0 miles southwest.

SHELTON

BROWN CREEK (Olympic National Forest)
22 units, trailers to 22', well, swimming, fishing, hiking trails.
Northwest of Shelton. US 101 7.5 miles north, Cty 242 5.3 miles northwest, FSR 23 8.7 miles north, FSR 2286 .5 miles east.

TAMPICO

AHTANUM (Dept. of Natural Resources)
11 campsites, drinking water, trail, creek, fishing.
West of Tampico. Head northwest out of Tampico along the North Fork Ahtanum Creek Road approximately 9 miles. Campground is on left.

AHTANUM MEADOWS (Dept. of Natural Resources)
7 campsites, creek.
West of Tampico. Head northwest out of Tampico along the North Fork Ahtanum Creek Road approximately 9 miles. Campground is on right.

CLOVER FLATS (Dept. of Natural Resources)
9 campsites, drinking water.
West of Tampico. Head northwest out of Tampico along the North Fork Ahtanum Creek Road approximately 11 miles. Turn left and proceed another 8 miles, staying right at the Y, to the campground.

GREEN LAKE (Dept. of Natural Resources)
6 campsites, fishing.
West of Tampico. Head northwest out of Tampico along the North Fork Ahtanum Creek Road approximately 18 miles to its junction with Darland Loop Road. Turn right and travel another 2 miles to campground.

SNOW CABIN (Dept. of Natural Resources)
8 campsites, creek, fishing, horse facilities.
West of Tampico. Head northwest out of Tampico along the North Fork Ahtanum Creek Road approximately 15.5 miles to campground.

TREE PHONES (Dept. of Natural Resources)
14 campsites, trail, horse facilities, creek.
West of Tampico. Head northwest out of Tampico along the North Fork Ahtanum Creek Road approximately 11.5 miles. Turn left and proceed another 5 miles to campground.

TONASKET

LYMAN LAKE (Okanogan National Forest)
6 units, trailers to 32', swimming, fishing.
Southeast of Tonasket. State 20 12.6 miles east, Cty 9455 13.0 miles southeast, Cty 3185 2.4 miles south.

WEST FORK SAN POIL (Okanogan National Forest)
8 units, trailers to 32', stream, fishing.
Southeast of Tonasket. State 20 12.6 miles east, Cty 9455 29.6 miles southeast, FSR 359 3.2 miles southeast.

TROUT LAKE

COLD SPRINGS (Gifford Pinchot National Forest)
3 tent units, no trailers, Mt. Adams Trailhead.
North of Trout Lake. State 141 .2 miles southeast, Cty 17 1.9 miles north, FSR 80 3.5 miles north, FSR 8040 8.0 miles north.

FORLORN LAKES (Gifford Pinchot National Forest)
7 units, trailers to 18', swimming, fishing.
West of Trout Lake. State 141 5.0 miles west, FSR 24 3 miles west, FSR 60 5.0 miles west, FSR 6040 2.5 miles north.

GOOSE LAKE (Gifford Pinchot National Forest)
19 units, no trailers, boat launch, swimming, fishing.
Southwest of Trout Lake. State 141 5.5 miles southwest, FSR 24 2.5 miles west, FSR 60 5.2 miles southwest.

ICE CAVE (Gifford Pinchot National Forest)
12 units, trailers to 18', no water, lava tube cave.
Southwest of Trout Lake. State 141 5.5 miles southwest, FSR 24 .9 miles west.

LEWIS RIVER (Gifford Pinchot National Forest)
3 tent units, no trailers, swimming, fishing, hiking trails.
Northwest of Trout Lake. State 141 1.4 miles west, FSR 88 12.3 miles northwest, FSR 8851 7.2 miles north, FSR 32 1 mile west, FSR 3241 3.0 miles west.

LITTLE GOOSE (Gifford Pinchot National Forest)
20 units, trailers to 18', piped water, stream, hiking trails.
Northwest of Trout Lake. State 141 5.5 miles southwest, FSR 24 10.1 miles northwest.

LITTLE GOOSE HORSE CAMP (Gifford Pinchot National Forest)
5 units, trailers to 18', piped water, stream, hiking, horse trails.
Northwest of Trout Lake. State 141 5.5 miles southwest, FSR 24 10.1 miles northwest.

MORRISON CREEK (Gifford Pinchot National Forest)
10 tent units, no trailers, Mt. Adams Trailhead.
North of Trout Lake. State 141 .2 miles southeast, Cty 17 1.9 miles north, FSR 80 3.5 miles north, FSR 8040 6.1 miles north.

MORRISON CREEK HORSE CAMP (Gifford Pinchot National Forest)
3 units, trailers to 18', Mt. Adams Trailhead.
North of Trout Lake. State 141 .2 miles southeast, Cty 17 1.9 miles north, FSR 80 3.5 miles north, FSR 8040 6.0 miles north.

SADDLE (Gifford Pinchot National Forest)
11 units, trailers to 18', huckleberry area.
Northwest of Trout Lake. State 141 5.5 miles southwest, FSR 24 18.3 miles northwest, FSR 2480 1.3 miles north.

SMOKEY CREEK (Gifford Pinchot National Forest)
4 units, trailers to 18', stream, hiking trails.
West of Trout Lake. State 141 5.5 miles southwest, FSR 24 4.5 miles north.

SOUTH (Gifford Pinchot National Forest)
9 units, trailers to 18', well, fishing, huckleberry area.
Northwest of Trout Lake. State 141 5.5 miles southwest, FSR 24 18.3 miles northwest, FSR 2480 .3 miles east.

STEAMBOAT LAKE (Gifford Pinchot National Forest)
3 units, lake – no motors, swimming, fishing, hiking trails.
Northwest of Trout Lake. State 141 1.5 miles west, FSR 88 12.6 miles northwest, FSR 8851 3.0 miles northwest, FSR 8854 2.5 miles south.

TWIN FALLS (Gifford Pinchot National Forest)
4 units, trailers to 18', on upper Lewis River, fishing, hiking, trails.
Northwest of Trout Lake. State 141 1.4 miles west, FSR 88 16.3 miles northwest, FSR 150 5.2 miles north.

WICKY SHELTER (Gifford Pinchot National Forest)
3 units, shelter, trailers to 18', stream, fishing, hiking trails.
North of Trout Lake. State 141 .5 miles north, US 12 1.0 mile north, FSR 80 3.5 miles, FSR 8040 1.5 miles north.

TWISP

FOGGY DEW (Okanogan National Forest)
13 units, no trailers, stream, fishing, hiking trails.
South of Twisp. State 20 2.2 miles east, State 153 11.7 miles south, Cty 1029 3.0 miles southwest, FSR 4340 4.1 miles west.

MYSTERY (Okanogan National Forest)
5 units, trailers to 18', river, fishing, hiking trails.
West of Twisp. Cty 9114 10.8 miles west, FSR 44 7.3 miles northwest.

ROADS END (Okanogan National Forest)
4 units, no trailers, river, fishing, hiking trails.
West of Twisp. Cty 9114 10.8 miles west, FSR 44 14.4 miles northwest.

SOUTH CREEK (Okanogan National Forest)
4 units, no trailers, fishing, hiking trails.
West of Twisp. Cty 9114 10.8 miles west, FSR 44 11.3 miles northwest.

USK

PANHANDLE (Colville National Forest)
11 units, trailers to 22', piped water, boat launch, fishing, water skiing, Box Canyon Reservoir.
North of Usk. Cty 91 .3 miles east, Cty 7 16.2 miles north.

WINTHROP

CAMP 4 (Okanogan National Forest)
5 units, trailers to 18', river, fishing.
Northeast of Winthrop. Cty 1213 6.6 miles north, FSR 51 11.3 miles northeast.

CHEWUCK (Okanogan National Forest)
4 units, trailers to 18', river, fishing.
Northeast of Winthrop. Cty 1213 6.6 miles north, FSR 51 2.6 miles northeast.

HARTS PASS (Okanogan National Forest)
5 tent units, no trailers.
Northwest of Winthrop. State 20 13.2 miles northwest, Cty 1163 6.9 miles northwest, FSR 5400 12.5 miles northwest.

HONEYMOON (Okanogan National Forest)
6 tent units, trailers to 18', stream, fishing.
Northwest of Winthrop. Cty 1213 6.6 miles north, FSR 383 11.7 miles northwest.

MEADOWS (Okanogan National Forest)
14 tent units, no trailers, stream, access to Alpine Meadows.
Northwest of Winthrop. State 20 13.2 miles northwest, Cty 9140 6.9 miles northwest, FSR 5400 13.5 miles northwest, FSR 500 .5 miles south.

THIRTY MILE (Okanogan National Forest)
10 tent units, trailers to 18', stream, fishing, hiking trails.
Northeast of Winthrop. Cty 1213 6.6 miles north, FSR 51 22.7 miles northeast.

OREGON CAMPGROUNDS

AZALEA

DEVILS FLAT (Umpqua National Forest)
6 tent units, stream, trails.
East of Azalea. Cty 36 18.2 miles east.

BEAVER

ALDER GLEN (BLM)
7 units, drinking water, swimming.
East of Beaver 15 miles on Nestucca access road.

DOVRE (BLM)
10 units, drinking water, swimming.
East of Beaver 21 miles on Nestucca access road.

FAN CREEK (BLM)
12 units, drinking water, swimming.
East of Beaver 24 miles on Nestucca access road.

ROCKY BEND (Siuslaw National Forest)
7 tent units, swimming, fishing, Nestucca River.
Southeast of Beaver. Cty 542 15.6 miles east.

BEND

BIG RIVER (Deschutes National Forest)
17 units, trailers to 22', Deschutes River, fishing.
Southwest of Bend. US 97 16.5 miles south, Cty 42 5 miles southwest.

DEVILS LAKE (Deschutes National Forest)
9 units, hike in, stream, fishing, trails.
Southwest of Bend. State 46 to Bachelor Butte Ski Area, campground is 8.5 miles further.

DILLON FALLS (Deschutes National Forest)
7 units, trailers okay, on Deschutes River, fishing, boat launch.
Southwest of Bend. State 46 6.5 miles southwest, FSR 41 3 miles southwest, FSR 700 .9 miles southeast.

IRISH & TAYLOR (Deschutes National Forest)
3 tent units, lake, fishing, trails, rough road.
Southwest of Bend. State 46 43 miles southwest FSR 4630 1 mile west, FSR 30600 2.5 miles southwest FSR 30600 7 miles west. Campground is 5.5 miles west of Little Cultus Lake along primitive roads.

LITTLE CULTUS (Deschutes National Forest)
10 units, trailers to 22', lake, fishing, swimming.
Southwest of Bend. State 46 43.6 miles southwest, FSR 4630 3.4 miles southwest, FSR 30600 1.6 miles west.

MALLARD MARSH (Deschutes National Forest)
17 units, trailers to 22', well, on Hosmer Lake, fishing.
West of Bend.   State 46   31.3 miles southwest, FSR 470   2.7 miles southeast.

ROSLAND (Deschutes National Forest)
9 units, trailers to 22', Little Deschutes River, swimming, fishing.
South of Bend. US 97 23 miles south, Cty 43 2 miles west.

SAND SPRINGS (Deschutes National Forest)
7 units, trailers to 22', no water, primitive.
Southeast of Bend. US 20 20 miles east, FSR 23 18.6 miles southeast.

SLOUGH (Deschutes National Forest)
5 units, trailers to 18', Deschutes River, fishing.
Southwest of Bend.   State 46   6.5 miles southwest, FSR 41   .5 miles southwest, FSR 20500 5 miles south.

SODA CREEK (Deschutes National Forest)
12 units, trailers to 22', on Sparks Lake, fishing.
West of Bend. State 46 25.2 miles southwest, FSR 400 .1 miles south.

SOUTH (Deschutes National Forest)
23 units, trailers to 22', Hosmer Lake, boat launch.
West of Bend.   State 46   31.3 miles southwest, FSR 470   2.8 miles southeast.

SWAMP WELLS (Deschutes National Forest)
5 units, trailers to 22', horse camp.
South of Bend. US 97 1.5 miles south, FSR 18 6 miles east, FSR 1810 5.5 miles south, FSR 1816 3.2 miles southeast.

TODD LAKE (Deschutes National Forest)
4 tent units, very scenic, walk-in, fishing.
West of Bend.   State 46   22.6 miles southwest, FSR 370   .4 miles northeast, hike-in .1 mile northwest.

TUMALO FALLS (Deschutes National Forest)
4 tent units, stream, fishing.
West of Bend. FSR 4601 13.2 miles west, FSR 4603 2.5 miles west.

BLUE RIVER

DUTCH OVEN (Willamette National Forest)
6 tent units, river, fishing, primitive.
East of Blue River. State 126 3 miles east, FSR 19 south around reservoir 14 miles.

HOMESTEAD (Willamette National Forest)
4 units, river, fishing, primitive.
East of Blue River. State 126 3 miles east, FSR 19 south around reservoir 15 miles.

ROARING RIVER (Willamette National Forest)
5 units, river, fishing.
East of Blue River. State 126 3 miles east, FSR 19 south around reservoir 19 miles.

TWIN SPRINGS (Willamette National Forest)
7 units, trailers okay, river, fishing.
East of Blue River. State 126 3 miles east, FSR 19 south around reservoir 18 miles.

BLY

CORRAL CREEK (Fremont National Forest)
5 units, trailers to 18', stream, fishing, remote site, trails nearby into Gearhart Mt. Wilderness.
East of Bly. State 140 1.4 miles southeast, Cty 1257 .5 miles north, FSR 348 14.6 miles east, FSR 3621 .5 miles northwest.

LOFTON RESERVOIR (Fremont National Forest)
17 units, trailers to 22', well water, good fishing, steep road.
Southeast of Bly. State 140 12.5 miles southeast, FSR 3715 7.6 miles south, FSR 3715-A 1.3 miles northeast.

BROOKINGS

LONG RIDGE (Siskiyou National Forest)
2 units, primitive.
East of Brookings. FSR 1376 to FSR 1917. This will take you to the campground.

BROTHERS

PINE MOUNTAIN (Deschutes National Forest)
4 units, tents, no water.
West of Brothers. State 20 10 miles west, FSR 2017 7 miles south.

BURNS

IDLEWILD (Malheur National Forest)
27 units, trailers okay, drinking water, group picnic area.
North of Burns. US 395 17 miles north.

ROCK SPRINGS (Malheur National Forest)
8 units, trailers okay, drinking water.
North of Burns. US 395 33.8 miles north, FSR 17 4.5 miles east, FSR 1836 1 mile southeast.

TAMARACK SPRING (Malheur National Forest)
3 units, trailers okay.
North of Burns. US 395 33.8 miles north, FSR 17 4.7 miles east, FSR 1601 1.1 mile north.

YELLOWJACKET (Malheur National Forest)
25 units, trailers to 22', lake, fishing.
Northwest of Burns. US 20 1 mile south, FSR 47 32 miles northwest, FSR 37 4 miles east, FSR 3745 .5 miles south.

BUTTE FALLS

IMNAHA (Rogue River National Forest)
4 units, stream, remote.
Northeast of Butte Falls. FSR 34 15 miles northeast, FSR 37 4 miles north.

PARKER MEADOWS (Rogue River National Forest)
6 units, trailers okay.
Northeast of Butte Falls. FSR 34 15 miles northeast, FSR 37 4 miles east.

SNOWSHOE (Rogue River National Forest)
East of Butte Falls. FSR 30 10 miles southeast, FSR 3065 7 miles northeast.

SOUTH FORK (Rogue River National Forest)
2 units, remote.
Northeast of Butte Falls. FSR 34 15 miles northeast.

CAMP SHERMAN

ABBOTT CREEK (Deschutes National Forest)
4 units, trailers to 18', fishing.
Northwest of Camp Sherman. FSR 1420 4 miles northwest, FSR 12 3 miles northwest, FSR 1280 .5 miles northwest.

CANDLE CREEK (Deschutes National Forest)
5 units, trailers to 18', stream, fishing.
North of Camp Sherman. FSR 14 10 miles north, FSR 980 3 miles north.

JACK CREEK (Deschutes National Forest)
5 units, trailers to 18', stream, fishing.
Northwest of Camp Sherman. FSR 1420 3.6 miles north, FSR 1425 2 miles northwest, FSR 1230 .5 miles west.

JACK LAKE (Deschutes National Forest)
2 units, lake – no motors, swimming, fishing, trails into Mt. Jefferson Wilderness.
Northwest of Camp Sherman. FSR 1420 4 miles north, FSR 1425 2 miles west, FSR 1230 1 mile northwest, FSR 1234 5 miles west.

LOWER CANYON CREEK (Deschutes National Forest)
4 units, trailers to 18', fishing, trails.
North of Camp Sherman. FSR 1420 5 miles north.

RIVERSIDE (Deschutes National Forest)
7 units, trailers to 22', stream.
South of Camp Sherman. FSR 900 1.4 miles south.

CAVE JUNCTION

BOLAN LAKE (Siskiyou National Forest)
12 units, trailers to 18', boat launch – no motors on lake, swimming, fishing.
South of Cave Junction. State 199 7 miles south, Cty 5070 4 miles east, Cty 5828 2 miles east, FSR 48 9 miles to FSR 4812, 4 miles east to spur road 040 to campground.

ONION CAMP (Siskiyou National Forest)
3 units, hiking, fishing, wilderness trailhead.
West of Cave Junction 17 miles.

CHEMULT

CORRAL SPRINGS (Winema National Forest)
5 units, trailers to 22', primitive.
Northwest of Chemult. US 97 2.7 miles north, FSR 2652A 1.9 miles west.

JACKSON CREEK (Winema National Forest)
12 units, trailers to 22', horse corral, hike into Yamsay Crater.
Southeast of Chemult. US 97 24.5 miles south, Cty 676 22.1 miles
northeast, FSR 3037 5.3 miles southeast.

CHILOQUIN

HEAD OF THE RIVER (Winema National Forest)
6 units, trailers to 32', primitive, fishing.
Northeast of Chiloquin. Cty 858 5 miles northeast, Cty 600 27 miles
northeast, FSR 3032 1 mile north.

COQUILLE

PARK CREEK (BLM)
12 units, water.
Southeast of Coquille. State 42 5 miles south, east to McKinley, Middle
Creek Road north 10 miles.

COTTAGE GROVE

SHARPS CREEK (BLM)
10 units, creek, swimming.
Southwest of Cottage Grove. Take Dorena/Culp Creek Road 12 miles, at
Culp Creek take Sharps Creek Road south 4 miles to campground.

COVE

MOSS SPRINGS (Wallowa-Whitman National Forest)
6 units, trailers to 22', picnic sites, hiking trails, creek.
East of Cove. Cty 602 1.5 miles southeast, FSR 6220 6.5 miles east.

CRESCENT/CRESCENT LAKE

CONTORTA POINT (Deschutes National Forest)
6 units, trailers to 22', Crescent Lake, fishing, swimming, water skiing.
Southwest of Crescent Lake. FSR 60 10.9 miles southwest, FSR 60280
1 mile southwest.

LAVA FLOW (Deschutes National Forest)
12 units, trailers to 22', on Davis Lake, excellent fishing.
Northwest of Crescent. Cty 61 9 miles west, FSR 46 9 miles north, FSR 850
2 miles north.

LITTLE DESCHUTES (Deschutes National Forest)
5 units, trailers to 22', well, fishing.
Southwest of Crescent. US 97 10 miles south, State 58 4.1 miles
northwest.

SUMMIT LAKE (Deschutes National Forest)
3 units, trailers to 22', lake, boat launch, swimming, fishing, trails.
Southwest of Crescent Lake. FSR 60 7.3 miles southwest, FSR 6010
6.7 miles west.

CULP CREEK

CEDAR CREEK (Umpqua National Forest)
8 units, trailers to 18', stream, fishing, swimming.
Southeast of Culp Creek. FSR 2149 5 miles southeast, Cty 36 6.3 miles
east.

LUNDPARK (Umpqua National Forest)
4 units, trailers to 18', stream, swimming, fishing.
Southeast of Culp Creek, FSR 2149 5 miles southeast, Cty 36 6.3 miles
east.

MINERAL (Umpqua National Forest)
2 units, stream, swimming, fishing.
Southeast of Culp Creek. Cty 202 .8 miles southeast, Cty 2235 10.5 miles
southeast, FSR 230 1.8 miles east.

CULVER

MONTY (Deschutes National Forest)
45 units, trailers to 22', piped water, Metolius River, fishing.
Northwest of Culver. County road 64 miles west, FSR 64 16 miles
northwest.

PERRY SOUTH (Deschutes National Forest)
63 units, trailers to 22', Lake Billy Chinook, boat launch, fishing, swimming.
Northwest of Culver. County road 64 miles west, FSR 64 5 miles northwest.

DALE

OLIVE LAKE (Umatilla National Forest)
6 units, trailers to 32', boat launch.
Southeast of Dale. US 395 1 mile northeast, FSR 55 .6 miles southeast,
FSR 10 26.3 miles southeast, FSR 420 .3 miles southwest.

TOLLBRIDGE (Umatilla National Forest)
7 units, creek, fishing, primitive.
Northeast of Dale. US 395 1 mile northeast, FSR 55 .6 miles southeast,
FSR 10 .1 miles southeast.

TROUGH CREEK (Umatilla National Forest)
Tent sites, primitive, no tables.
Northeast of Dale. US 395 1 mile northeast, FSR 55 .6 miles southeast,
FSR 10 13.9 miles southeast.

DETROIT

CLEATOR BEND (Willamette National Forest)
8 units, trailers okay, river, swimming, fishing, nearby trails, primitive.
Northeast of Detroit. FSR 46 9.6 miles northeast.

ELK LAKE (Willamette National Forest)
14 tent units, stream, boat launch, fishing, hiking.
North of Detroit. Take the Elkhorn-Elk Lake Road #2209 14 miles north.

PIETY ISLAND (Willamette National Forest)
12 tent units, swimming, fishing, water skiing, on Detroit Reservoir, primitive, boat in.
Southwest of Detroit. By boat 1.1 miles southwest on lake.

UPPER ARM (Willamette National Forest)
5 units, some trailers, boating, swimming, fishing, water skiing.
Northeast of Detroit. FSR 46 1 mile northeast. On Breitenbush Arm of Detroit Lake.

DRAIN

GUNTER (BLM)
8 units, water.
North of Drain. Leave State 99 on Smith River County Road, head north 8 miles to campground.

DUFUR

EIGHTMILE CROSSING (Mt. Hood National Forest)
14 units, trailers to 18', fishing, creek.
Southwest of Dufur. Cty 1 12 miles southwest, FSR 44 4.3 miles west, FSR 105 .6 miles north.

FIFTEEN MILE (Mt. Hood National Forest)
4 units, trailers to 18', creek.
Southwest of Dufur. State 197 2 miles south, Cty 118 14 miles west, FSR 205 9 miles west.

KNEBAL SPRING (Mt. Hood National Forest)
6 units, trailers to 22', creek.
West of Dufur. Cty 1 12 miles southwest, FSR 44 4.3 miles west, FSR 105 4 miles north, FSR 16 1 mile southwest.

LOWER CROSSING (Mt. Hood National Forest)
2 units, trailers to 18', fishing, stream.
Southwest of Dufur. Cty 1 12 miles southwest, FSR 44 4 miles west, FSR 167 1 mile north.

PEBBLE FORD (Mt. Hood National Forest)
5 units, trailers to 18', stream.
Southwest of Dufur. Cty 1 12 miles southwest, FSR 44 5 miles west, FSR 3550 .5 miles south.

ELGIN

WOODLAND (Umatilla National Forest)
6 units, trailers to 22'.
Northwest of Elgin. State 204 16.6 miles northwest.

ENTERPRISE

BUCKHORN (Wallowa-Whitman National Forest)
6 units, picnic sites, spring.
Northeast of Enterprise. State 3 16 miles north, FSR 46 51 miles east to campground.

COYOTE (Wallowa-Whitman National Forest)
Northeast of Enterprise. State 3 16 miles north, FSR 46 40 miles north.

DOUGHERTY SPRINGS (Wallowa-Whitman National Forest)
10 units, trailers okay, stream, fishing, hiking.
Northeast of Enterprise. State 3 16 miles north, FSR 46 38 miles north.

VIGNE (Wallowa-Whitman National Forest)
12 units, trailers to 22', well water, stream, picnic sites.
Northeast of Enterprise. State 82 3 miles east, Cty 799 21.6 miles north, FSR 4620 6.5 miles north, FSR 4625 11 miles east.

ESTACADA

ALDER FLAT (Mt. Hood National Forest)
6 tent units, hike in, on Clackamas River, hiking, trails.
Southeast of Estacada. State 224 25.8 miles southeast, Trail 574 .7 miles west.

BIG SLIDE LAKE (Mt. Hood National Forest)
2 tent units, hike in, trails, swimming, fishing, lake.
Southeast of Estacada. State 224 26.7 miles southeast, FSR S4600 3.7 miles south, FSR S6300 5.4 miles south, FSR S708/6340 2.9 miles southwest, FSR S708A 2 miles to Dickey Creek Trailhead. Trail 533 4 miles to lake.

BREITENBUSH LAKE (Mt. Hood National Forest)
5 units, trailers to 18', swimming, fishing, trails, lake.
Southeast of Estacada. State 224 27 miles southeast, FSR 4600 28.6 miles south, FSR 4220 8.4 miles east. Access road is primitive and unmaintained. No motors allowed on the lake.

CAMP TEN (Mt. Hood National Forest)
2 units, trailers to 18', fishing, trails, lake.
Southeast of Estacada. State 224 27 miles southeast, FSR 4600 21.8 miles south, FSR 806/4690 8.2 miles southeast, FSR 4220 6.1 miles south. No motors allowed on the lake.

EAST TWIN LAKE (Mt. Hood National Forest)
3 units, hike in, fishing, swimming.
Southeast of Estacada. State 224 26.7 miles southeast, FSR 4600 3.7 miles south, FSR S6300 5.4 miles, FSR S708/6340 8.0 miles southwest, FSR S739/6341 3.5 miles southwest, Trails 551, 558 and 573 10 miles to campground.

FRAZIER FORK (Mt. Hood National Forest)
5 tent units, trails.
Southeast of Estacada. State 224 27 miles southeast, FSR S5700 7.5 miles east, FSR S5800 7 miles northeast, FSR S457/4610 2.2 miles northeast, FSR S456/4610240 4.2 miles west. Primitive road. Trailhead to Rock Lakes.

FRAZIER TURN AROUND (Mt. Hood National Forest)
8 tent units, trails.
Southeast of Estacada. State 224 27 miles southeast, FSR S5700 7.5 miles east, FSR S5800 7 miles northeast, FSR S457/4610 2.2 miles northeast, FSR S456/4610240 4.2 miles west. Primitive road. Trailhead to Rock Lakes.

HAMBONE SPRINGS (Mt. Hood National Forest)
7 tent units, creek.
Southeast of Estacada. State 224 7 miles southeast, FSR S403/4611
7.9 miles southeast, FSR S469/4610 17.2 miles southeast.

HIGH ROCK SPRING (Mt. Hood National Forest)
7 tent units, drinking water, creek.
Southeast of Estacada. State 224 27 miles southeast, FSR S5700 7.5
miles east, FSR S5800 9 miles northeast, FSR 3457 1.5 miles northwest.

HORSESHOE LAKE (Mt. Hood National Forest)
4 tent units, swimming, fishing, lake.
Southeast of Estacada. State 224 27 miles southeast, FSR S4600 21.8
miles south, FSR S806/4690 8.2 miles southeast, FSR S4200 8.3 miles
south.

LAKE LENORE (Mt. Hood National Forest)
2 tent units, fishing, lake, trails, hike in.
Southeast of Estacada. State 224 27 miles southeast, FSR S4600 3.7
miles south, FSR S6300 5.4 miles south, FSR S708/6340 2.9 miles
southwest, FSR 708A 2.0 miles, Trails 553 and 555 6 miles. Steep trail
to lake.

LOOKOUT SPRINGS (Mt. Hood National Forest)
6 units, trailers to 18', trails.
Southeast of Estacada. State 224 7.6 miles southeast, FSR S403/4611
7.9 miles southeast, FSR S469/4610 5.1 miles northeast.

LOWER LAKE (Mt. Hood National Forest)
11 tent units, creek, trails.
Southeast of Estacada. State 224 27 miles southeast, FSR 4600 21.8
miles south. FSR S806/4690 8.2 miles southeast, FSR 4200 4.5 miles
south.

NORTH FORK CROSSING (Mt. Hood National Forest)
11 units, trailers to 18', stream, fishing.
Southeast of Estacada. State 224 7 miles southeast, FSR S403/4611 8
miles southeast, FSR S457 .5 miles northwest. Located on North Fork of
Clackamas River.

OLALLIE MEADOW (Mt. Hood National Forest)
7 units, trailers to 18', no water, trails.
Southeast of Estacada. State 224 27 miles southeast, FSR S4600 8.2
miles southeast, FSR S42 1.4 miles south.

PANSY LAKE (Mt. Hood National Forest)
3 tent units, lake, hike in.
Southeast of Estacada. State 224 27 miles southeast, FSR S4600 3.7
miles south, FSR S6300 5.4 miles south, FSR 739/6341 3.5 miles south,
FSR S708/6340 3.5 miles southeast, Trail 551 1 mile.

PAUL DENNIS (Mt. Hood National Forest)
24 units, trailers to 18', lake, boat launch – no motors, swimming, fishing,
hiking trails.
Southeast of Estacada. State 224 27 miles southeast, FSR 4600 21.8
miles south, FSR 806/4690 8.2 miles southeast, FSR S4200 6.3 miles
south.

RIVERFORD (Mt. Hood National Forest)
10 units, trailers to 18', creek, swimming, fishing, trails.
Southeast of Estacada. State 224 27 miles southeast, FSR S4600 3.5 miles south.

SHINING LAKE (Mt. Hood National Forest)
11 tent units, fishing, trails, hike-in.
Southeast of Estacada. State 224 27 miles southeast, FSR S5700 7.5 miles east, FSR S5800 7.6 miles northeast, FSR S457/4610 2.2 miles northeast, FSR S456/4610240 7.1 miles to Indian Ridge Trail, 4 miles to campground.

TWIN SPRINGS (Mt. Hood National Forest)
6 tent units, trails, cold water spring.
Southeast of Estacada. State 224 7 miles southeast, FSR S403/4611 8 miles southeast, FSR S469/4610 10.9 miles southeast.

WELCOME LAKE (Mt. Hood National Forest)
2 tent units, fishing, hiking, lake, hike in.
Southeast of Estacada. State 224 27 miles southeast, FSR S4600 3.7 miles south, FSR S6300 14.5 miles south, Trail 554 4 miles to lake.

WEST TWIN LAKE (Mt. Hood National Forest)
2 tent units, hike in, lake, swimming, fishing, trails.
Southeast of Estacada. State 224 27 miles southeast, FSR S4600 3.7 miles south, FSR S6300 5.4 miles south, FSR S708/6340 8 miles southwest, FSR S739/6341 3.5 miles southwest, Trails 551, 558 and 573 10 miles to campground.

FISH LAKE

BEAVER DAM (Rogue River National Forest)
4 tent units, creek, closed if without volunteer maintenance.
South of Fish Lake. State 140 1.5 miles west, FSR 37 1.2 miles north.

DALEY CREEK (Rogue River National Forest)
5 tent units, creek, closed if without volunteer maintenance.
South of Fish Lake. State 140 1.5 miles west, FSR 37 1.3 miles north.

WILLOW PRAIRIE (Rogue River National Forest)
9 units.
Northwest of Fish Lake. State 140 3 miles west, FSR 3735 2 miles north.

FLORENCE

LODGEPOLE (Siuslaw National Forest)
3 units, trailers to 22', water, on Siltcoos River.
South of Florence. US 101 7.6 miles south, FSR 1070 1 mile west.

FORT ROCK

CABIN LAKE (Deschutes National Forest)
14 units, trailers okay, piped water.
North of Fort Rock. FSR 18 9.8 miles north. Isolated.

CHINA HAT (Deschutes National Forest)
14 units, trailers okay, piped water.
North of Fort Rock. FSR 18 22.7 miles north.

FOX

BEECH CREEK (Malheur National Forest)
4 units, trailers to 18', water.
Southeast of Fox. US 395 6 miles south.

FRENCHGLEN

FISH LAKE (BLM)
20 units, lake, hiking trails.
Southeast of Frenchglen. Located 18 miles east of State 205 out of Frenchglen.

JACKMAN PARK (BLM)
4 units, hiking.
Southeast of Frenchglen. Located 20 miles east of State 205 out of Frenchglen.

PAGE SPRINGS (BLM)
15 units, hiking.
Southeast of Frenchglen. Located 2 miles east of State 205 out of Frenchglen.

GALICE

BIG SLIDE (BLM)
Campsites, toilets, on Rogue River, hike-in or boat-in.
Northwest of Galice. Access along river.

DOE CREEK (BLM)
Campsites, toilets, boat-in only.
Northwest of Galice. River access only.

NORTH RUSSIAN CREEK (BLM)
Campsites, toilets, hike-in or boat-in.
Northwest of Galice. Access along river.

RAINIE FALLS (BLM)
Campsites, toilets, hike-in or boat-in.
Northwest of Galice. Access along river.

WHISKEY CREEK (BLM)
Campsites, toilets, hike-in or boat-in.
Northwest of Galice. Access along river.

WILDCAT/SOUTH RUSSIAN CREEK (BLM)
Campsites, toilets, boat-in only.
Northwest of Galice. Rogue River access only.

GARDINER

SMITH RIVER FALLS (BLM)
8 units.
Northeast of Gardiner. US 101 1.5 miles north, Smith River Road 27 miles east.

GLIDE

COOLWATER CAMP (Umpqua National Forest)
7 units, trailers to 18', well, river, swimming, fishing, trails.
East of Glide. State 138, Cty 17 13.1 miles southeast, FSR 27 2.9 miles east.

HEMLOCK LAKE (Umpqua National Forest)
15 units, trailers to 22', lake – no motors, swimming, fishing, 8 mile loop trail.
Southeast of Glide. Cty 17 13.1 miles east, FSR 27 18.3 miles east, FSR 495 .5 miles south.

WHITE CREEK (Umpqua National Forest)
1 unit, trailers to 22', well, river, swimming, fishing, trails, walk-in sites.
East of Glide. Cty 17 13.1 miles east, FSR 27 4 miles east, FSR 2792 2 miles east.

GOLD BEACH

ELKO (Siskiyou National Forest)
3 tent units, primitive.
Southeast of Gold Beach. US 101 1.6 miles south, Cty 635 6.1 miles southeast, FSR 3680 9.9 miles southeast, FSR 3680 .5 miles east.

FAIRVIEW (Siskiyou National Forest)
1 unit, trailer okay, primitive.
Southeast of Gold Beach. FSR 3680 to campground.

LOBSTER CREEK (Siskiyou National Forest)
5 units, water, boat ramp.
East of Gold Beach. FSR 331 8.5 miles.

WILDHORSE (Siskiyou National Forest)
3 tent units, water, primitive.
Northeast of Gold Beach. US 101 1.6 miles south, Cty 635 6.1 miles southeast, FSR 3680 16.4 miles northeast, FSR 3318 4.6 miles northeast.

GOVERNMENT CAMP

BARLOW CREEK (Mt. Hood National Forest)
5 units, trailers to 18', creek, fishing, trails.
Northeast of Government Camp. US 26 2 miles east, State 35 4.5 miles north, FSR S30/3530 4.2 miles southeast.

BARLOW CROSSING (Mt. Hood National Forest)
6 units, trailers to 18', stream, fishing.
Southeast of Government Camp. US 26 2 miles east, State 35 4.5 miles north, FSR S30/3530 5.2 miles southeast.

DEVILS HALF ACRE (Mt. Hood National Forest)
4 units, trailers to 18', stream.
Northeast of Government Camp. US 26 2 miles east, State 35 4.5 miles north, FSR S30/3530 1 mile east.

FIR TREE (Mt. Hood National Forest)
5 tent units, creek, trailhead to Vida Lake.
South of Government Camp. US 26 1 mile east, FSR S32/2613 5.1 miles southwest.

GRINDSTONE (Mt. Hood National Forest)
3 units, trailers to 18', creek.
Northeast of Government Camp. US 26 2 miles east, State 35 4.5 miles north, FSR S30/3530 4.2 miles southeast.

KINZEL LAKE (Mt. Hood National Forest),
5 tent units, creek, swimming, trails.
Southwest of Government Camp. US 26 1 mile east, FSR S32/2613 10.6 miles southwest. Primitive road.

LINNEY CREEK (Mt. Hood National Forest)
4 tent units, creek, fishing, trails.
Southwest of Government Camp. US 26 15 miles southeast, FSR S42/4220 4 miles south, FSR S457/4610 11.7 miles southwest, FSR 407 4.3 miles north.

MEDITATION POINT (Mt. Hood National Forest)
3 tent units, lake, swimming, fishing, boat in.
South of Government Camp. US 26 15 miles southeast, FSR S42/4220 8 miles south, FSR S5700 6 miles west, boat 1 mile north.

SUMMIT LAKE (Mt. Hood National Forest)
6 tent units, lake – no motors, swimming.
South of Government Camp. US 26 15 miles southeast, FSR S42/4220 13 miles south, FSR 601/5730 1 mile southeast, FSR 633/4661140 1 mile west.

WHITE RIVER STATION (Mt. Hood National Forest)
5 units, trailers to 18', creek, fishing.
Southeast of Government Camp. US 26 2 miles east, State 35 4.5 miles north, FSR 30/3530 7.2 miles northeast.

HAINES

NORTH FORK ANTHONY CREEK (Wallowa-Whitman National Forest)
4 tent sites, fishing, hiking.
Northeast of Haines. State 30 4 miles north, FSR 73 11 miles east.

HALFWAY

DUCK LAKE (Wallowa-Whitman National Forest)
3 units, hiking.
North of Halfway. Off State 86 – 39 miles north of Halfway on FSR 3980.

McBRIDE (Wallowa-Whitman National Forest)
5 units, trailers to 18', creek.
Northwest of Halfway. Cty 442 5 miles northwest, FSR 72 2.1 miles west, FSR 7710 2.5 miles west.

TWIN LAKES (Wallowa-Whitman National Forest)
6 tent sites, lake, fishing.
North of Halfway. Take FSR 66 35 miles north to campground.

HEBO

CASTLE ROCK (Siuslaw National Forest)
6 units, well, fishing, stream.
Southeast of Hebo. State 22 4.1 miles southeast.

SOUTH LAKE (Siuslaw National Forest)
3 units, lake.
East of Hebo. State 22 east, FSR 1400 to FSR 1428138. Campground is 7.2 miles from Hebo.

HINES

BUCK SPRING (Ochoco National Forest)
8 units, trailers to 22', piped water.
Northwest of Hines. US 20 24.5 miles west, Cty 1938 12.6 miles north, FSR 1938 7.4 miles north, FSR 2034 .9 miles northwest, FSR 2094 1 mile west.

IDLEYLD PARK

APPLE CREEK (Umpqua National Forest)
8 units, trailers to 22', N. Umpqua River, fishing.
East of Idleyld Park. State 138 22.5 miles east.

BOULDER FLAT (Umpqua National Forest)
16 units, trailers to 22', N. Umpqua River, fishing, trails.
East of Idleyld Park. State 138 31.8 miles east.

BUNKER HILL (Umpqua National Forest)
4 tent units, Lemolo Lake, swimming, fishing, water skiing.
East of Idleyld Park. State 138 42.4 miles east, FSR 2610 5.4 miles north, FSR 268 .3 miles southeast.

CALAMUT LAKE (Umpqua National Forest)
1 tent unit, lake – no motors, swimming, fishing, primitive, hike-in.
East of Idleyld Park. State 138 54.3 miles east, FSR 2500 7.2 miles northeast, FSR 2165 2 miles northwest, Trail 1494 1.2 miles north.

CLEARWATER FALLS (Umpqua National Forest)
10 units, trailers to 18', waterfall, fishing, primitive.
East of Idleyld Park. State 138 46.2 miles east, FSR 2735 .3 miles east.

EAST LEMOLO (Umpqua National Forest)
6 units, trailers to 22', primitive fishing camp, swimming, water skiing.
Northeast of Idleyld Park. State 138 49.4 miles east, FSR 2610 3.2 miles north, FSR 2666 2.3 miles northeast.

INLET (Umpqua National Forest)
14 units, trailers to 22', lake, trails.
East of Idleyld Park. State 138 49.4 miles east, FSR 2610 3.2 miles north, FSR 2666 2.7 miles northeast.

ISLAND (Umpqua National Forest)
7 units, trailers to 22', N. Umpqua River, fishing.
East of Idleyld Park. State 138 19 miles east.

KELSAY VALLEY (Umpqua National Forest)
2 units, trailers to 18', stream, fishing, trails, primitive.
East of Idleyld Park. State 138 50.4 miles east, FSR 2500 4.7 miles northeast, FSR 2507 .3 miles east.

LEMOLO TWO FOREBAY (Umpqua National Forest)
4 units, trailers to 18', lake, swimming, fishing, primitive.
East of Idleyld Park. State 138 35.2 miles east, FSR 268 3.9 miles
northeast, FSR 2640 1.2 miles west.

STEAMBOAT FALLS (Umpqua National Forest)
13 units, trailers to 22', stream – no fishing, swimming.
Northeast of Idleyld Park. State 138 23.5 miles east, Cty 249 to FSR 38 to
campground. (7 miles northeast of Steamboat)

THIELSEN (Umpqua National Forest)
3 tent units, stream, primitive.
East of Idleyld Park. State 138 50.1 miles east.

TOKETEE LAKE (Umpqua National Forest)
33 units, trailers to 22', river, fishing, boat launch, water skiing, trails.
East of Idleyld Park. State 138 35.2 miles east, FSR 34 1.4 miles northeast.

TWIN LAKES (Umpqua National Forest)
6 tent units, lake – no motors, swimming, fishing, primitive, hike-in.
East of Idleyld Park. State 138 36 miles east, FSR 4770 9.5 miles
southeast, Trail 1500 2 miles west.

WHITEHORSE FALLS (Umpqua National Forest)
5 tent units, stream, fishing.
East of Idleyld Park. State 138 42.4 miles east.

WILLIAMS CREEK (Umpqua National Forest)
2 tent units, stream, swimming, fishing.
Northeast of Idleyld Park. State 138 7.8 miles southeast, FSR 4710 8.5
miles northeast.

IMNAHA

HAT POINT (Wallowa-Whitman National Forest)
2 units, hiking, outstanding view.
From Imnaha take FSR 4240 to Hat Point. Campground is 54 miles
northeast of Joseph.

SACAJAWEA (Wallowa-Whitman National Forest)
6 units, view.
From Imnaha take FSR 4240 to Hat Point. Campground is at the end of
FSR 315 just past the observation point.

SADDLE CREEK (Wallowa-Whitman National Forest)
4 tent sites, hiking, view.
Southeast of Imnaha. Take FSR 4240 11 miles to campground.

JACKSONVILLE

COOK AND GREEN (Rogue River National Forest)
4 units, trailers to 18', well, stream, fishing, horse trail, closed if without
volunteer maintenance.
Southwest of Jacksonville. State 238 8 miles southwest, Cty 859 17
miles southwest, FSR 41S01 5 miles southwest.

HARR POINT CAMP (Rogue River National Forest)
5 tent units, swimming, fishing, trails.
Southwest of Jacksonville. State 238 8 miles southwest, Cty 859 17 miles southwest.

HUTTON (Rogue River National Forest)
3 tent units, stream, remote.
Southwest of Jacksonville. State 238 8 miles southwest, Cty 859 17 miles southwest, near southern tip of lake.

LATGANA COVE CAMP (Rogue River National Forest)
5 tent units, swimming, fishing, trails.
Southwest of Jacksonville. State 238 8 miles southwest, Cty 859 15 miles southwest, FSR 1075 1 mile east.

TIPSU TYEE CAMP (Rogue River National Forest)
5 tent units, lake, swimming, fishing, trails.
Southwest of Jacksonville. State 238 8 miles southwest, Cty 859 16 miles southwest.

JOHN DAY

CANYON MEADOWS (Malheur National Forest)
34 units, boat launch, hiking, fishing.
Southeast of John Day. US 395 10 miles south, FSR 15 5 miles southeast, FSR 1520 5 miles northeast.

RAY COLE (Malheur National Forest)
4 units, trailers to 22', stream.
Southeast of John Day. US 395 10 miles south, FSR 15 3 miles southeast, FSR 1510 1 mile north.

WICKIUP (Malheur National Forest)
15 units, trailers to 18', stream, fishing.
Southeast of John Day. US 395 10 miles south, FSR 15 8 miles southeast.

JOSEPH

HURRICANE CREEK (Wallowa-Whitman National Forest)
6 units, trailers to 18', stream, trails into Eagle Cap Wilderness.
Southwest of Joseph. County road 3.5 miles southwest, FSR 8205 .6 miles south.

JUNTURA

CHUKAR PARK (BLM)
15 units, hiking, trails.
North of Juntura. West of Juntura take the road to Beulah Reservoir 6 miles to campground.

KENO

SURVEYOR (BLM)
12 campsites, water.
West of Keno. State 66 5 miles west, follow signs to Howard Prairie Reservoir, 10 miles to campground.

TOPSY (BLM)
12 campsites.
West of Keno. State 66 5 miles west.

KLAMATH FALLS

COLDSPRINGS (Winema National Forest)
2 tent units, primitive, trailhead access to Sky Lakes Wilderness.
Northwest of Klamath Falls. State 140 27.5 miles northwest, FSR 3561
8.5 miles north.

FOURMILE LAKE (Winema National Forest)
29 units, well water, boat launch, trailhead access to Sky Lakes Wilderness.
Northwest of Klamath Falls. State 140 33.1 miles northwest, FSR 3661
5.5 miles north.

ODESSA (Winema National Forest)
5 units, trailers to 22', primitive boat launch, stream.
North of Klamath Falls. State 140 21 miles north, FSR 3639 1 mile north.

SEVENMILE MARSH (Winema National Forest)
2 tent units, trailhead access to Sky Lakes Wilderness.
West of Klamath Falls. Cty 531 west 4.5 miles, FSR 3334 6.5 miles to
campground.

LA GRANDE

BIKINI BEACH (Wallowa-Whitman National Forest)
5 units, trailers to 22', river.
Southwest of La Grande. I-84 9 miles southwest, State 244 13 miles
southwest, FSR 51 4.5 miles south.

GRANDVIEW (Wallowa-Whitman National Forest)
4 units, trailers to 22', water, view.
North of La Grande. I-84 20 miles west, Cty 31 20 miles north, FSR 3120
3.2 miles south.

RIVER (Wallowa-Whitman National Forest)
6 units, trailers to 22', well water, picnic sites, river.
Southwest of La Grande. I-84 9 miles southwest, State 244 13 miles
southwest, FSR 51 9 miles south.

SHERWOOD FOREST (Wallowa-Whitman National Forest)
5 units, trailers to 22', river.
Southwest of La Grande. I-84 9 miles southwest, State 244 13 miles
southwest, FSR 51 6.5 miles south.

UTOPIA (Wallowa-Whitman National Forest)
2 units, trailers to 18', river.
Southwest of La Grande. I-84 9 miles southwest, State 244 13 miles
southwest, FSR 51 5.5 miles south.

WOODLEY (Wallowa-Whitman National Forest)
7 units, trailers to 22', picnic sites, river, hiking trails.
Southwest of La Grande. I-84 9 miles southwest, State 244 13
miles southwest, FSR 51 11 miles south, FSR 5125 6 miles southeast.

La PINE

BULL BEND (Deschutes National Forest)
3 tent units, on Deschutes River, fishing.
Northwest of LaPine. US 97 2.4 miles northeast, Cty 43 8 miles west,
FSR 4370 1.5 miles southwest.

COW MEADOW (Deschutes National Forest)
17 units, trailers to 22', on Deschutes River and Crane Prairie Reservoir,
fishing.
Northwest of La Pine. US 97 2.4 miles northeast, Cty 43 10 miles west,
Cty 42 10 miles west, Cty 46 7 miles north, FSR 620 1.5 miles
southeast.

CRANE PRAIRIE (Deschutes National Forest)
32 units, trailers to 22', well, lake, fishing.
Northwest of La Pine. US 97 2.4 miles northeast, Cty 43 10 miles west,
Cty 42 6 miles west, FSR 4270 4.5 miles north.

FALL RIVER (Deschutes National Forest)
12 units, trailers to 22', stream, fly fishing only.
Northwest of La Pine. US 97 2.4 miles northeast, Cty 43 7.8 miles west,
FSR 4350 2.1 miles northwest, Cty 42 .8 miles northeast.

LITTLE LAVE LAKE (Deschutes National Forest)
11 units, trailers to 22', fishing.
Northwest of La Pine. US 97 2.4 miles northeast, Cty 43 10 miles west,
Cty 42 10 miles west, FSR 46 13.5 miles north, FSR 500 1 mile east.

McKAY CROSSING (Deschutes National Forest)
10 units, trailers to 22', stream, fishing.
Northeast of La Pine. US 97 5 miles north, Cty 21 3 miles southeast,
FSR 2120 2.1 miles east.

NORTH COVE (Deschutes National Forest)
6 tent units, lake, fishing, trails, hike-in or boat-in only.
East of La Pine. US 97 5 miles north, Cty 21 13.1 miles east, boat 1.4
miles north or follow Trail 55. Located on northwest shore of Paulina Lake.

NORTH DAVIS CREEK (Deschutes National Forest)
15 units, trailers to 22', lake, boat launch, fishing.
West of La Pine. US 97 2.4 miles northeast, Cty 43 10 miles west,
Cty 42 10 miles west, Cty 46 4 miles south. At Wickiup Reservoir.

NORTH TWIN (Deschutes National Forest)
9 units, trailers to 22', lake – no motors, fishing, swimming.
West of La Pine. US 97 2.4 miles northeast, Cty 43 10 miles west,
Cty 42 4 miles west, FSR 4260 .1 mile southwest, campground road
.2 miles south.

PRINGLE FALLS (Deschutes National Forest)
12 units, trailers to 22', on Deschutes River, fishing.
Northwest of La Pine. US 97 2.4 miles northeast, Cty 43 7.2 miles west,
FSR 30500 .7 miles northeast.

RESERVOIR (Deschutes National Forest)
28 units, trailers to 22', on Wickiup Reservoir, fishing.
West of La Pine, US 97 2.4 miles northeast, Cty 43 10 miles west, Cty 42 10 miles west, Cty 46 5.8 miles south, FSR 44 1.7 miles east.

SHEEP BRIDGE (Deschutes National Forest)
18 units, trailers to 22', well water, on Deschutes River at Wickiup Reservoir.
West of La Pine. US 97 2.4 miles northeast, Cty 43 10 miles west, Cty 42 5.3 miles west, FSR 4260 .6 miles west, FSR 60070 .7 miles west.

WARM SPRINGS (Deschutes National Forest)
5 tent units, lake, trails, fishing, boat-in.
East of La Pine. US 97 5 miles north, Cty 21 15.8 miles north. On northeast shore of Paulina Lake.

WEST CULTUS (Deschutes National Forest)
15 tent units, lake, fishing, swimming, trails, hike-in or boat-in only.
Southwest of La Pine. US 46 44.3 miles southwest, FSR 4635 1.6 miles northwest, boat 2.7 miles west.

WICKIUP BUTTE (Deschutes National Forest)
6 units, trailers to 22', lake, boat launch, swimming, fishing.
West of La Pine. US 97 2.4 miles northeast, Cty 43 7.2 miles west, FSR 44 7.2 miles southwest, FSR 4260 1.5 miles northwest.

WYETH (Deschutes National Forest)
2 units, trailers to 22', river, fishing.
Northwest of La Pine. US 97 2.4 miles northeast, Cty 43 7.7 miles west, FSR 4370 .1 miles south.

LAKEVIEW

COTTONWOOD MEADOWS (Fremont National Forest)
26 units, trailers okay, lake, swimming, fishing.
Northwest of Lakeview. State 140 20 miles west, FSR 387 5 miles northeast.

DEEP CREEK (Fremont National Forest)
9 units, trailers to 22', stream, good fishing, remote site.
Southeast of Lakeview. US 395 5.4 miles north, State 140 6.5 miles east, FSR 391 16.1 miles south.

DOG LAKE (Fremont National Forest)
11 units, trailers to 18', piped water, lake, nearby boat launch, fishing.
Southwest of Lakeview. State 140 5.6 miles wet, Cty W60 7 miles south, FSR 4017 13 miles west.

MUD CREEK (Fremont National Forest)
6 units, trailers to 18', piped water, stream, good fishing.
Northeast of Lakeview. US 395 5.4 miles north, State 140 6.5 miles east, FSR 3615 6.1 miles north.

WILLOW CREEK (Fremont National Forest)
11 units, trailers to 22', well water, stream, good fishing, remote site.
Southeast of Lakeview. US 395 5.4 miles north, State 140 6.5 miles east, FSR 391 10 miles south.

LOSTINE

FRENCH CAMP (Wallowa-Whitman National Forest)
4 tent sites, stream, fishing, hiking.
South of Lostine. Off State 82 follow Cty 551 7 miles south, FSR 8210 7 miles south.

LILLYVILLE (Wallowa-Whitman National Forest)
2 units, trailers okay, stream, trailheads to wilderness.
South of Lostine. Off State 82 follow Cty 551 7 miles south, FSR 8210 8 miles south.

SHADY (Wallowa-Whitman National Forest)
16 units, trailers to 18', river, trailheads to wilderness.
South of Lostine. Leave State 82 taking Cty 551 7 miles, FSR 8210 10 miles south.

TWO PAN (Wallowa-Whitman National Forest)
9 tent units, river, trailheads to wilderness.
South of Lostine. Off State 82 follow Cty 551 7 miles south, FSR 8210 11 mile south.

WILLIAMSON (Wallowa-Whitman National Forest)
14 tent units, river, trailheads to wilderness.
South of Lostine. Off State 82 follow Cty 551 7 miles south, FSR 8210 4 miles south.

LOWELL

DOLLY VARDEN (Willamette National Forest)
5 tent units, hiking, fishing, swimming.
Northeast of Lowell. State 58 to Fall Creek Road #18, 12 miles northeast of Lowell.

MARIAL

BATTLE BAR (BLM)
Campsites on Rogue River, toilet, boat-in.
East of Marial. River access only.

BIG WINDY (BLM)
Campsites, toilets, boat-in only.
Southeast of Marial. Rogue River access only.

BRUSHY BAR (Siskiyou National Forest)
8 tent units, water, stream, swimming, fishing, trails, hike-in or boat-in, primitive.
West of Marial. Cty 375 5.9 miles north, Trail 1160 8 miles northeast. Hike-in or Rogue River access only.

DITCH CREEK (BLM)
Campsites, toilets, hike-in or boat-in.
East of Marial. Access along river.

DULOG (BLM)
Campsites, toilets, hike-in or boat-in.
East of Marial. Access along river.

EAST MULE CREEK (BLM)
Campsites, toilets, hike-in or boat-in.
East of Marial. Access along river.

HEWITT CREEK (BLM)
Campsites, toilets, boat-in only.
East of Marial. Rogue River access only.

HORSESHOE BEND (BLM)
Campsites, toilets, hike-in or boat-in only.
East of Marial. Access along river.

JENNY CREEK (BLM)
Campsites, toilets, boat-in only.
Southeast of Marial. Rogue River access only.

KELSEY CREEK (BLM)
Campsites, toilets, hike-in or boat-in.
East of Marial. Access along river.

LITTLE WINDY (BLM)
Campsites, toilets, boat-in only.
Southeast of Marial. Rogue River access only.

LONG GULCH (BLM)
Campsites, toilets, boat-in only.
East of Marial. Rogue River access only.

MEADOW CREEK (BLM)
Campsites, toilets, hike-in or boat-in.
East of Marial. Access along river.

TUCKER FLAT (BLM)
12 units, toilets, hard to find.
North of Marial. Take Marial Road out of Galice to campground.

WEST MULE CREEK (BLM)
Campsites, toilets, hike-in or boat-in.
North of Marial. Access along river.

MAUPIN

BLUE HOLE (BLM)
6 units, picnic units for handicapped.
North of Maupin. Sherar's Bridge road 4 miles north.

CLEAR CREEK (Mt. Hood National Forest)
6 units, trailers to 18', creek, fishing.
Northwest of Maupin. State 216 25 miles west, FSR S401/2130 3 miles north.

KEEPS MILL (Mt. Hood National Forest)
4 tent units, creek, fishing.
Northwest of Maupin. State 216 24 miles west, FSR 483/2120 3 miles north.

McCUBBINS GULCH (Mt. Hood National Forest)
5 units, trailers to 18', stream, primitive.
Northwest of Maupin. State 216 24.5 miles northwest, FSR S508/2110 1 mile east.

McKENZIE BRIDGE

ALDER SPRINGS (Willamette National Forest)
7 tent units, stream, trail to lake, fishing.
East of McKenzie Bridge. State 126 4.3 miles east, State 242 8.2 miles east.

FISH LAKE (Willamette National Forest)
16 units, trailers okay, near lava beds.
Northeast of McKenzie Bridge. State 126 22.4 miles northeast, FSR 1374 .1 miles west. Lake recedes in summer.

FROG (Willamette National Forest)
4 tent units, stream, trails.
Northeast of McKenzie Bridge. State 242 13 miles east of its junction with State 126, FSR 250 .3 miles to campground. Obsidian trail to Pacific Crest Trail.

LAKES END (Willamette National Forest)
17 tent units, on Smith Reservoir, swimming, fishing, boat-in only.
Northwest of McKenzie Bridge. State 126 13.2 miles northwest, FSR 1477 3.3 miles northwest, Boat 1.8 miles north.

LIMBERLOST (Willamette National Forest)
12 tent units, creek, fishing.
East of McKenzie Bridge. State 126 4.3 miles east, State 242 .5 miles east.

OLALLIE (Willamette National Forest)
19 units, trailers okay, river, fishing.
Northeast of McKenzie Bridge. State 126 11.1 miles northeast.

SCOTT LAKE (Willamette National Forest)
20 tent units, lake, boating, swimming, fishing, outstanding view, trails, hike-in.
Northeast of McKenzie Bridge. State 126 3.4 miles east, State 242 14.6 miles northeast, FSR 1532 .4 miles southwest, walk to tent units.

MEDICAL SPRINGS

TWO COLOR (Wallowa-Whitman National Forest)
14 units, trailers to 22', drinking water, stream, hiking, trails.
East of Medical Springs. FSR 6700 5.5 miles southeast, FSR 6700 10.2 miles east, FSR 7755 1.2 miles northeast.

MEHAMA

SHADY COVE (Willamette National Forest)
9 tent units, river, fishing.
East of Mehama. State 22 9 miles east, Cty 967 15.3 miles east, FSR S80 1.1 miles east, FSR S81 2.1 miles east.

MITCHELL

COTTONWOOD (Ochoco National Forest)
3 units, trailers to 22', primitive.
Southeast of Mitchell. US 26 10 miles east, FSR 1240 6.9 miles south, FSR 127 6.1 miles southeast, FSR 127 .4 miles south.

MT. VERNON

BILLY FIELDS (Malheur National Forest)
6 units, trailers to 22', stream, fishing, near Cedar Grove Botanical Area.
Southwest of Mt. Vernon. US 26 10 miles west, FSR 145 7 miles south.

MAGONE LAKE (Malheur National Forest)
20 units, picnic area, trailers okay, water, boat launch, fishing, swimming, hiking trails.
Northeast of Mt. Vernon. US 395 9 miles north, FSR 36 8 miles northeast, FSR 3620 1.5 miles north, FSR 3618 1 mile west.

OREGON MINE CAMPGROUND (Malheur National Forest)
3 units, trailers to 22', stream, fishing, hiking.
Southwest of Mt. Vernon. US 26 10 miles west, FSR 21 14 miles south, FSR 2170 1 mile northwest.

NESKOWIN

NESKOWIN CREEK (Siuslaw National Forest)
12 tent units in Cascade Head Experimental Forest.
Southeast of Neskowin. US 101 1.5 miles southeast, Cty 12 4.7 miles southeast, FSR 12131 .1 miles west.

NORTHBEND

SPINREEL (Siuslaw National Forest)
25 units, trailers to 22', stream, dune access.
Northwest of North Bend. US 101 8 miles northwest, county road 1 mile northwest. Approximately 2 miles from Ten-Mile Lake off 101.

OAKRIDGE

BLAIR LAKE (Willamette National Forest)
9 units, lake – no motors, well, fishing, swimming.
Northeast of Oakridge. Cty 149 1 mile east, FSR 24 8 miles northeast, FSR 1934 7.4 miles northeast, FSR 733 1.5 miles east.

CAMPERS FLAT (Willamette National Forest)
5 units, trailers okay, river, well, fishing.
Southeast of Oakridge. State 58 2.2 miles southeast, Cty 360 .5 miles southeast, FSR 21 20 miles south.

FERRIN (Willamette National Forest)
7 units, trailers okay, river, fishing.
West of Oakridge. State 58 2.1 miles west.

HAMPTON (Willamette National Forest)
5 units, trailers okay, on Lookout Point Reservoir, boating, swimming, fishing, water skiing.
West of Oakridge. State 58 to upper end of Lookout Point Reservoir, 9 miles west of Oakridge.

HARRALSON HORSE CAMP (Willamette National Forest)
5 units, Waldo Lake Recreation Area, boat launch, swimming, fishing, trails.
Southeast of Oakridge. State 58 23.1 miles southeast, FSR 5897 10.5 miles northeast, FSR 5898 1.3 miles northwest.

INDIGO LAKE (Willamette National Forest)
5 units, lake, swimming, fishing, hike-in.
Southeast of Oakridge. State 58 2.2 miles southeast, Cty 360 .5 miles southeast, FSR 21 38.4 miles southeast, FSR 2154 3.2 miles south, Trail 3649 2 miles south.

INDIGO SPRINGS (Willamette National Forest)
3 units, creek, fishing.
Southeast of Oakridge. State 58 2.2 miles southeast, Cty 360 .5 miles southeast, FSR 21 29 miles southeast.

OPAL LAKE (Willamette National Forest)
1 unit, lake, fishing, nearby trails.
Southeast of Oakridge. State 58 2.2 miles southeast, Cty 360 .5 miles southeast, FSR 21 38 miles southeast, FSR 2154 2 miles south, FSR 398 .5 miles north.

RHODODENDRON ISLAND (Willamette National Forest)
3 tent units, lake – speed limits, swimming, fishing, boat-in only.
Southeast of Oakridge. State 58 23.1 miles southeast, FSR 5897 6.2 miles northeast, FSR 5896 2.5 miles northwest, Boat 1.6 miles northwest.

SACANDAGA (Willamette National Forest)
19 units, trailers okay, fishing.
Southeast of Oakridge. State 58 26 miles southeast.

SALT CREEK FALLS (Willamette National Forest)
4 units, some trailers, 286' waterfall, fishing, hiking.
Southeast of Oakridge. State 58 20.7 miles southeast.

SECRET (Willamette National Forest)
6 units, river, fishing.
Southeast of Oakridge. State 58 2.2 miles southeast, Cty 360 .5 miles southeast, FSR 21 18.3 miles south.

TAYLOR BURN (Willamette National Forest)
15 units, trailers okay, piped water, fishing, trails to high country lakes.
Northeast of Oakridge. State 58 23.1 miles northeast, FSR 5897 10.5 miles northeast, FSR 5898 1.7 miles northwest, FSR 517 6.8 miles northwest.

TIMPANOGAS LAKE (Willamette National Forest)
10 units, trailers okay, lake – no motors, well, swimming, fishing, trails.
Southeast of Oakridge. State 58 2.2 miles southeast, Cty 360 .5 miles southeast, FSR 21 38 miles southeast, FSR 2154 3 miles south, FSR 399 5 miles south.

PAISLEY

CAMPBELL LAKE (Fremont National Forest)
15 units, trailers to 22', well water, lake, swimming, good fishing, no motors on lake.
Southwest of Paisley. Cty 422 1 mile west, FSR 331 22.7 miles west, FSR 2823 3 miles south, FSR 3403 3.4 miles north.

DEAD HORSE LAKE (Fremont National Forest)
21 units, trailers to 22', well water, lake – no motors, fishing, trails.
Southwest of Paisley. Cty 422 1 mile west, FSR 331 22.7 miles west, FSR 2823 3 miles south, FSR 3403 4.4 miles south.

HAPPY CAMP (Fremont National Forest)
9 units, trailers to 18', piped water, Dairy Creek, good fishing.
Southwest of Paisley. Cty 422 1 mile south, FSR 330 20.3 miles south, FSR 2823 2.4 miles south, FSR 3675 1 mile west.

LEE THOMAS (Fremont National Forest)
7 units, trailers to 22', well water, stream, good fishing.
Southwest of Paisley. Cty 422 1 mile west, FSR 331 26.9 miles.

MARSTERS SPRING (Fremont National Forest)
10 units, trailers to 22', well water, stream, good fishing.
South of Paisley. Cty 422 1 mile west, FSR 330 7.1 miles south.

SANDHILL CROSSING (Fremont National Forest)
5 units, trailers to 18', well water, stream, good fishing.
Southwest of Paisley. Cty 422 1 mile west, FSR 331 25.2 miles.

PARKDALE

CLOUD CAP SADDLE (Mt. Hood National Forest)
3 tent units, no water, trails.
Southwest of Parkdale. State 35 8 miles south, FSR S12/2612 11.7 miles west. Starting point for climbing Mt. Hood or hiking Timberline Trail.

GIBSON PRAIRIE HORSE CAMP (Mt. Hood National Forest)
7 units, trailers to 18', trails.
Northeast of Parkdale. Cty 428 2 miles northeast, State 35 3 miles north, FSR N107/1700 15 miles southeast.

HOOD RIVER MEADOWS TRAILHEAD (Mt. Hood National Forest)
3 tent units, stream, fishing, trails.
Southwest of Parkdale. State 35 25 miles southeast. Trailhead to Mt. Hood Wilderness.

INDIAN SPRINGS (Mt. Hood National Forest)
4 tent units, stream, trails.
Northwest of Parkdale. State 281 6 miles north, Cty 501 6 miles southwest, FSR N13/1300 5 miles west, FSR N18/1810 8 miles northwest.

RAINY LAKE (Mt. Hood National Forest)
4 tent units, lake, swimming, fishing, trails.
Northwest of Parkdale. State 281 6 miles north, FSR N205/2820 10 miles west. Lake is ¼ mile from campground.

TILLY JANE (Mt. Hood National Forest)
10 tent units, stream, trails, hike-in.
Southwest of Parkdale. State 35 8 miles south, FSR S12/2612 11 miles
west. Historic area.

WAHTUM LAKE (Mt. Hood National Forest)
5 units, trailers to 18', lake, swimming, fishing, trails.
Northwest of Parkdale. State 281 6 miles north, Cty 501 5 miles
southwest, FSR N13/1300 5 miles west, FSR N18/1810 8 miles
northwest, FSR N20/2820620. Located ¼ mile from lake. Trail to 8
additional tent units at lake.

PAULINA

BIG SPRING (Ochoco National Forest)
4 units, piped water, primitive.
South of Paulina. Cty 112 3.5 miles east, Cty 113 6.5 miles north, FSR 142
2 miles north, FSR 154 1 mile north.

FRAZIER (Ochoco National Forest)
5 units, primitive.
Northeast of Paulina. Cty 112 3.5 miles east, Cty 113 2.2 miles north, Cty
135 10 miles east, FSR 158 6.3 miles east, FSR 1548 1.1 miles northeast.

MUD SPRING (Ochoco National Forest)
3 units, trailers to 22'.
Northeast of Paulina. Cty 112 4 miles east, Cty 113 2.2 miles north, Cty
135 10.2 miles east, FSR 158 4.2 miles east, FSR 127 6 miles north.

SUGAR CREEK (Ochoco National Forest)
10 units, trailers to 22', hiking trails, stream.
Northeast of Paulina. Cty 112 3.5 miles east, Cty 113 6.5 miles north, FSR
142 .8 miles north, FSR 158 1 mile east.

WOLF CREEK (Ochoco National Forest)
6 units, trailers to 22', stream.
Northeast of Paulina. Cty 112 3.5 miles east, Cty 113 6.6 miles north, FSR
142 1.6 miles north, FSR 154 .2 miles north.

PENDLETON

UMATILLA FORKS (Umatilla National Forest)
19 tent units, 5 units for trailers to 22', horse trails, river.
East of Pendleton. Cty N32 32 miles east, FSR 32 .6 miles southeast.

PORT ORFORD

BUTLER BAR (Siskiyou National Forest)
10 units, trailers to 18', river, swimming, fishing.
East of Port Orford. US 101 3 miles north, Cty 208 7.4 miles southeast,
FSR 5325 11.2 miles southeast.

ELK LAKE (Siskiyou National Forest)
3 units, trailers to 18', lake – no floating devices allowed, swimming, fishing.
East of Port Orford. US 101 3 miles north, Cty 208 7.4 miles southeast,
FSR 5325 16.7 miles southeast.

McGRIBBLE (Siskiyou National Forest)
5 tent units, stream, primitive.
Southeast of Port Orford. US 101 3 miles north, Cty 208 7.4 miles southeast, FSR 5325 2.8 miles southeast, FSR 5502 .5 miles south, FSR 020 .5 miles.

POWERS

MYRTLE GROVE (Siskiyou National Forest)
5 tent units, river, swimming, fishing, primitive.
Southeast of Powers. Cty 219 4.2 miles southeast, FSR 33 10.4 miles south.

ROCK CREEK (Siskiyou National Forest)
6 units, creek, swimming, fishing, trails, primitive.
South of Powers, Cty 219 4.2 miles southeast, FSR 33 13 miles south, FSR 3347 1.3 miles southwest.

SQUAW LAKE (Siskiyou National Forest)
7 units, trailers okay, lake – no floating devices, swimming, fishing, trails.
Southeast of Powers. Cty 219 4.2 miles southeast, FSR 33 12.6 miles south, FSR 3348 around the Coquille River Falls Research Natural Area then west 4.6 miles.

PRAIRIE CITY

CRESCENT (Malheur National Forest)
4 tent units, stream.
Southeast of Prairie City. Cty 14 8.3 miles southeast, FSR 14 8.5 miles south.

DIXIE (Malheur National Forest)
11 units, trailers to 22', well water.
Northeast of Prairie City. US 26 7 miles southeast, FSR 1220 .5 miles north.

ELK CREEK (Malheur National Forest)
6 units, trailers to 18', fishing, N. Fork Malheur River.
Southeast of Prairie City. Cty 14 8.3 miles southeast, FSR 13 16 miles southeast, FSR 16 1.3 miles south.

INDIAN SPRINGS (Malheur National Forest)
7 units, trailers to 18', primitive, trails.
South of Prairie City. FSR 14 22 miles southeast, FSR 16 11.3 miles west, FSR 1640 6.5 miles north.

LITTLE CRANE (Malheur National Forest)
5 units, trailers to 18', stream, fishing.
Southeast of Prairie City. Cty 14 8.3 miles southeast, FSR 13 16 miles south, FSR 16 5.7 miles south.

McNAUGHTON SPRING (Malheur National Forest)
4 units, trailers to 22', stream.
South of Prairie City. Cty 60 6.6 miles south, FSR 6001 1.8 miles south.

MIDDLE FORK (Malheur National Forest)
11 units, trailers to 22', Middle Fork John Day River, fishing.
Northeast of Prairie City. US 26 11.5 miles northeast, Cty 20 5 miles northwest.

NORTH FORK MALHEUR (Malheur National Forest)
5 units, trailers okay, river, fishing.
Southeast of Prairie City. Cty 14 8.3 miles southeast, FSR 13 16 miles southeast, FSR 16 2 miles south, FSR 1675 2.7 miles south.

SLIDE CREEK (Malheur National Forest)
1 unit, trailers to 22', stream.
South of Prairie City. Cty 60 6.6 miles south, FSR 6001 2.1 miles south.

STRAWBERRY (Malheur National Forest)
11 units, trailers to 22', trailhead to Strawberry Mountain Wilderness.
South of Prairie City. Cty 60 6.6 miles south, FSR 6001 4.4 miles south.

TROUT FARM (Malheur National Forest)
9 units, trailers to 18', stream, pond, fishing.
Southeast of Prairie City. Cty 14 8.3 miles southeast, FSR 14 6.9 miles south.

PRINEVILLE

COUGAR (Ochoco National Forest)
6 units, trailers to 22', stream, fishing.
Northeast of Prineville. US 26 26 miles northeast, FSR 1356 .1 miles south.

DEEP CREEK (Ochoco National Forest)
6 units, trailers to 22', piped water, fishing.
East of Prineville. US 26 16.7 miles east, Cty 123 8.5 miles northeast, FSR 142 23.6 miles southeast, FSR 1426 .1 miles south.

DOUBLE CABIN (Ochoco National Forest)
2 units, trailers okay, stream.
Southeast of Prineville. State 380 29 miles southeast, FSR 1729 9 miles south, FSR 1887 4 miles east, FSR 1887-E .3 miles east.

ELK HORN (Ochoco National Forest)
4 units, trailers okay, piped water, fishing.
Southeast of Prineville. State 380 34 miles southeast, FSR 1728 4.3 miles southeast.

OCHOCO PICNIC GROUND (Ochoco National Forest)
6 units, water, creek, hiking trails.
East of Prineville. US 26 18 miles east, FSR 22 8.5 miles at junction with FSR 2610.

PINE CREEK (Ochoco National Forest)
2 units, piped water, primitive.
Northeast of Prineville. State 380 29 miles southeast, FSR 1729 9 miles south, FSR 1727 .3 miles east, FSR 1729A .1 miles north.

WILEY FLAT (Ochoco National Forest)
5 campsites, piped water, primitive.
Southeast of Prineville. State 380 34 miles southeast, FSR 1728 9.8 miles south, FSR 1728B 1 mile west.

PROSPECT

HUCKLEBERRY MOUNTAIN (Rogue River National Forest)
15 units, trailers okay.
Northeast of Prospect. FSR 60 4 miles northeast.

MILL CREEK (Rogue River National Forest)
8 units, trailers to 22', stream, fishing, closed if without volunteer maintenance.
North of Prospect. State 62 2.6 miles north, FSR 3247 1 mile east.

NATURAL BRIDGE (Rogue River National Forest)
21 units, trailers to 22', river, fishing, trails, river flows underground here.
North of Prospect. State 62 9.9 miles north, FSR 3106 1 mile west.

RIVER BRIDGE (Rogue River National Forest)
6 units, stream, fishing.
North of Prospect. State 62 4 miles north, FSR 3103 1 mile north.

REEDSPORT

NOEL RANCH (Siuslaw National Forest)
5 tent units, on Smith River, boat launch.
Northeast of Reedsport. US 101 1.4 miles north, State 48 8.5 miles northeast.

REMOTE

BEAR CREEK (BLM)
17 units.
East of Remote. State 42 8 miles east.

RICHLAND

EAGLE CREEK (Wallowa-Whitman National Forest)
10 units, stream, fishing, trailers to 22'.
Northwest of Richland. Cty 833 8.1 miles northwest, FSR 7735 14 miles northwest, FSR 7700 7 miles northwest.

EAGLE FORKS (Wallowa-Whitman National Forest)
7 units, trailers to 18', drinking water, picnic sites, trail.
Northwest of Richland. Cty 833 8.1 miles northwest, FSR 7735 2.7 miles northwest.

ROGUE RIVER

ELDERBERRY FLAT (BLM)
10 campsites.
North of Rogue River. Take the road to Wimer 19 miles, campground is on the left.

ROSEBURG

EMILE (BLM)
4 units, swimming.
Northeast of Roseburg. State 138 18 miles northeast, Little River Road east 15 miles to campground.

SALEM

ELKHORN VALLEY (BLM)
23 units, water, swimming.
East of Salem. State 22 24 miles east, Elkhorn Road north 10 miles.

SCAPPOOSE

SCAPONIA (BLM)
7 units, drinking water, stream.
Northwest of Scappoose. Campground is 18 miles along the road leading to Spitzenberg/Pittsburgh out of Scappoose.

SELMA

SIX MILE (Siskiyou National Forest)
3 units, primitive.
West of Selma. Cty 5070 2 miles west, FSR 4103 7 miles west.

SENECA

BIG CREEK (Malheur National Forest)
14 units, trailers to 22', well water.
East of Seneca FSR 16 20.5 miles east, FSR 162E .5 miles north.

MURRAY (Malheur National Forest)
6 units, trailers to 18', stream, fishing.
East of Seneca FSR 16 19 miles east, FSR 1513 2.6 miles north. (5 miles from Strawberry Mountain Wilderness)

PARISH CABIN (Malheur National Forest)
27 units, trailers to 22', fishing.
East of Seneca FSR 16 12 miles east.

STARR (Malheur National Forest)
25 units, trailers to 18', water.
North of Seneca US 395 9.1 miles north.

SILVER LAKE

EAST BAY (Fremont National Forest)
10 units, trailers to 22', well water, lake, nearby boat launch, swimming, fishing.
South of Silver Lake. State 31 .5 miles west, FSR 2833 13.2 miles south, FSR 2823-D 1.5 miles west.

SILVER CREEK MARSH (Fremont National Forest)
8 units, trailers to 22', well water, stream, fishing.
South of Silver Lake. State 31 1 mile west, FSR 288 9.7 miles south, FSR 2919 .2 miles southwest.

THOMPSON RESERVOIR (Fremont National Forest)
22 units, trailers to 22', well water, swimming, boat ramp, excellent fishing.
South of Silver Lake. State 31 1 mile west, FSR 288 13.7 miles south, FSR 3024 1.1 mile east.

SISTERS

BLACK PINE SPRING (Deschutes National Forest)
4 units, trailers to 18', spring.
South of Sisters. FSR 16 9 miles south.

DRIFTWOOD (Deschutes National Forest)
16 units, trailers to 18', lake – no motors, swimming, fishing, trails.
South of Sisters. FSR 16 17 miles south, FSR 900 1 mile south.

GRAHAM CORRAL (Deschutes National Forest)
30 units, trailers to 18', piped water, trails.
Northwest of Sisters. US 20 4.5 miles northwest, FSR 1012 1 mile
southwest, FSR 300 1 mile northwest, FSR 340 1 mile west.

LAVA CAMP LAKE (Deschutes National Forest)
12 units, trailers to 22', lake, swimming, fishing, trails.
West of Sisters. State 242 17 miles west, FSR 900 1 mile southeast.

ROUND LAKE (Deschutes National Forest)
5 tent units, lake – no motors, boat launch, swimming, fishing, trails.
Northwest of Sisters. US 20 12 miles northwest, FSR 12 1 mile north,
FSR 1210 5 miles northwest.

THREE CREEKS LAKE (Deschutes National Forest)
10 units, trailers to 18', lake, swimming, fishing.
South of Sisters. FSR 16 18 miles south.

THREE CREEKS MEADOW (Deschutes National Forest)
28 units, trailers to 18', creek, trails.
South of Sisters. Cty 16 16 miles south.

WHISPERING PINE (Deschutes National Forest)
8 units, trailers, trailers to 22', creek, fishing.
Southwest of Sisters. State 242 6 miles west, FSR 1018 5 miles south.

SIXES

SIXES RIVER (BLM)
19 units, trails.
East of Sixes. Head east out of Sixes along river for approximately 10
miles to campground.

SPRAY

FAIRVIEW (Umatilla National Forest)
5 units, trailers to 18', water.
Northeast of Spray. State 287 12.6 miles northeast, FSR 400 .5 miles
west.

STEAMBOAT

SCARED MAN (BLM)
10 units, river, swimming.
North of Steamboat. Take Camton County Road left 4 miles to campground.

SUMPTER

DEER CREEK (Wallowa-Whitman National Forest)
8 tent units, fishing, picnic area.
East of Sumpter. State 7 6 miles east, FSR 6530 3 miles north.

McCULLY FORKS (Wallowa-Whitman National Forest)
5 units, trailers to 18', creek.
Take Cty 520 3.5 miles past Sumpter to campground.

MILLERS LANE (Wallowa-Whitman National Forest)
7 units, trailers to 18', swimming, fishing, water skiing.
Southeast of Sumpter. State 220 5 miles southeast, FSR 2226 3.5 miles southeast.

SOUTHWEST OVERFLOW (Wallowa-Whitman National Forest)
5 units, trailers to 18', Phillips Lake, swimming, fishing, water skiing, boat launch.
Southeast of Sumpter. State 220 5 miles southeast, FSR 2226 2.6 miles southeast.

SUNRIVER

BESSON CAMP (Deschutes National Forest)
5 units, trailers okay, on Deschutes River, boat launch.
Near Sunriver. Leave US 97 at Sunriver to head left at Y across Harper Bridge, turn right on FSR 41, 1.5 miles north, FSR 240 1 mile east.

SUTHERLIN

TYEE (BLM)
11 units, water, swimming.
Northwest of Sutherlin. State 138 northwest 12 miles to Bullock Bridge, Cty 57 north .5 miles to campground.

TAFT

NORTH CREEK (Siuslaw National Forest)
11 units, swimming, fishing, stream.
Southeast of Taft. US 101 3.1 miles south, State 229 5.1 miles southeast, FSR 727 5.3 miles north.

SCHOONER CREEK (Siuslaw National Forest)
5 tent units, well, fishing.
Northeast of Taft. US 101 .1 miles south, Cty 106 6.8 miles northeast.

TALENT

WRANGLE (Rogue River National Forest)
5 units.
South of Talent. FSR 22 to FSR 20 to FSR 2030, campground is 16 miles south of Talent.

TILLER

BOULDER CREEK (Umpqua National Forest)
8 units, trailers to 18', well, swimming, fishing.
Northeast of Tiller. State 227 .3 miles southeast, Cty 46 6.2 miles northeast, FSR 284 7.7 miles northeast.

BUCKEYE LAKE (Umpqua National Forest)
3 tent units, lake, swimming, fishing, hike-in.
Northeast of Tiller. State 227 .3 miles southeast, Cty 46 6.2 miles northeast, FSR 284 20.4 miles northeast, FSR 2830 3.3 miles southeast, Trail 1575 1.5 miles southeast, Trail 1578 .5 miles southeast.

BUNCH GRASS MEADOWS (Umpqua National Forest)
Campsite/Shelter.
East of Tiller. State 227 .3 miles southeast, Cty 46 5 miles northeast, FSR 293 3.7 miles east, FSR 300 .7 miles south, FSR 3014 2.5 miles, FSR 3034 3 miles south.

CAMP COMFORT (Umpqua National Forest)
6 units, trailers to 18', stream, swimming, fishing, trails.
Northeast of Tiller. State 227 .3 miles southeast, Cty 46 6.2 miles northeast, FSR 284 17.9 miles northeast, FSR 2739 2.6 miles northeast.

CLIFF LAKE (Umpqua National Forest)
4 tent units, lake, swimming, fishing, hike-in.
Northeast of Tiller. State 227 .3 miles southeast, Cty 46 6.2 miles northeast, FSR 284 20.4 miles northeast, FSR 2830 5.3 miles southeast, Trail 1575 1.5 miles southeast, Trail 1578 .8 miles southeast.

COVER (Umpqua National Forest)
6 units, trailers to 18', stream, swimming, fishing, trails.
Northeast of Tiller. State 227 .3 miles southeast, Cty 46 5.8 miles northeast, FSR 29 13.6 miles east.

CRIPPLE CAMP (Umpqua National Forest)
3 units, primitive, hike-in.
Northeast of Tiller. State 227 .3 miles southeast, Cty 46 5 miles northeast, FSR 293 22.0 miles east, FSR 2933 6.7 miles east, Trail 1435 .7 miles northeast.

DUMONT CREEK (Umpqua National Forest)
5 units, trailers to 18', stream, fishing, swimming.
Northeast of Tiller. State 227 .3 miles southeast, Cty 46 6.2 miles northeast, FSR 284 5.4 miles northeast.

FISH LAKE (Umpqua National Forest)
6 tent units, lake, trails to 2 lakes & hikers campground, hike-in.
Northeast of Tiller. State 227 .3 miles southeast, Cty 46 6.2 miles northeast, FSR 284 20.4 miles northeast, FSR 2830 1.7 miles southeast, FSR 2840 .3 miles northeast, Trail 1570 3.7 miles southeast. Shelters.

MUD LAKE (Umpqua National Forest)
1 tent unit/shelter.
Northeast of Tiller. State 227 .3 miles southeast, Cty 46 6.2 miles northeast, FSR 284 18.4 miles northeast, FSR 2739 13.7 miles northeast, FSR 2715 1.1 miles northwest.

ROCKY RIDGE (Umpqua National Forest)
1 tent unit/shelter, trails.
Northeast of Tiller. State 227 .3 miles southeast, Cty 46 6.2 miles
northeast, FSR 284 20.4 miles northeast, FSR 2830 1.7 miles southeast,
FSR 2840 8.3 miles northeast.

THREEHORN (Umpqua National Forest)
6 units, trailers to 22', well.
Southeast of Tiller. State 227 12.7 miles southeast.

WHISKEY CAMP (Umpqua National Forest)
2 tent units, primitive, trails.
Southeast of Tiller. State 227 .3 miles southeast, Cty 46 5 miles
northeast, FSR 293 3.7 miles east, FSR 300 .7 miles south, FSR 3014 8.7
miles southeast.

TYGH VALLEY

LITTLE BADGER (Mt. Hood National Forest)
2 units, trailers to 22', creek, fishing.
Northwest to Tygh Valley. Cty 213 3 miles west, Cty 241 4.5 miles west,
FSR 308/2700 2.5 miles west, FSR 3012A .2 miles south.

UKIAH

BEAR WALLOW CREEK (Umatilla National Forest)
10 units, trailers to 32'.
Northeast of Ukiah. State 244 11 miles southwest.

FRAZIER (Umatilla National Forest)
29 units, trailers to 32', stream.
Northeast of Ukiah. State 244 10.5 miles east, FSR 5226 .5 miles south,
FSR 20 .2 miles east.

LANE CREEK (Umatilla National Forest)
10 units, trailers to 32'.
Northeast of Ukiah. State 244 10.5 miles east.

NORTH FORK JOHN DAY (Umatilla National Forest)
7 units, trailers to 22', river, trails.
Southeast of Ukiah. FSR 52 38.5 miles southeast.

UNION

NORTH FORK CATHERINE (Wallowa-Whitman National Forest)
5 units, trailers to 22', stream, hiking.
Southeast of Union. State 203 10 miles southeast, FSR 7700 and 7785
4 miles east.

UNITY

ELDORADO (Wallowa-Whitman National Forest)
2 units, trailers to 18', stream.
Southeast of Unity. US 26 10 miles southeast, FSR 1684 2 miles
southwest.

ELK CREEK (Wallowa-Whitman National Forest)
Campsites, creek.
Southwest of Unity. FSR 6005 10 miles southwest.

LONG CREEK (Wallowa-Whitman National Forest)
2 units, trailers to 18', creek.
South of Unity. FSR 16 9 miles south.

MAMMOTH SPRINGS (Wallowa-Whitman National Forest)
3 units, trailers to 18', creek.
Southwest of Unity. FSR 6005 10 miles southwest, FSR 2640 1.5 miles west.

STEVENS CAMP (Wallowa-Whitman National Forest)
Campsites, stream, trails.
Southwest of Unity. FSR 6005 7 miles west.

WALDPORT

CANAL CREEK (Siuslaw National Forest)
12 units, trailers to 22', stream, well.
Southeast of Waldport. State 34 7.6 miles east, FSR 3462 4.1 miles south.

MAPLES (Siuslaw National Forest)
7 units, trailers to 18', on Alsea River, swimming, fishing.
Southeast of Waldport. State 34 18.8 miles east, Cty 33 3.0 miles south, Cty 32 1.2 miles west.

WALLOWA

BOUNDARY (Wallowa-Whitman National Forest)
12 tent units, creek, trailhead to wilderness.
South of Wallowa, Cty 515 5 miles south, FSR 8250-040 2 miles south.

WAMIC

BADGER LAKE (Mt. Hood National Forest)
4 tent units, lake, creek, swimming, fishing.
Northwest of Wamic. Cty 226 6 miles west, FSR 408/4800 11 miles southwest, FSR 339/4860 10 miles northwest, FSR 340/4860140 5 miles northwest.

BONNEY CROSSING (Mt. Hood National Forest)
5 tent units, creek, fishing.
Northwest of Wamic. Cty 226 6 miles west, FSR 408/4800 1 mile west, FSR 466/4810 2 miles northwest, FSR 3010 1.4 miles north.

BONNEY MEADOWS (Mt. Hood National Forest)
6 units, trailers to 22', stream, fishing, trails.
Northwest of Wamic. Cty 226 6 miles west, FSR 408/4800 14.7 miles southwest, FSR 338/4891 5.9 miles north.

BOULDER LAKE (Mt. Hood National Forest)
3 tent units, lake – no motors, swimming, fishing, hike-in.
Northwest of Wamic. Cty 226 6 miles west, FSR 408/4800 12.2 miles
southwest, FSR 446/4880 5.7 miles west, Trail 463 .5 miles west.

CAMP WINDY (Mt. Hood National Forest)
2 tent units, fishing.
Northwest of Wamic. Cty 226 6 miles west, FSR 408/4800 11 miles
southwest, FSR 339/4860 12.3 miles northwest.

FOREST CREEK (Mt. Hood National Forest)
9 units, trailers to 22', creek, fishing.
Southwest of Wamic. Cty 226 6 miles west, FSR 408/4800 12.6 miles
southwest, FSR 415 1 mile southeast, FSR 30/3530 .2 miles south.

JEAN LAKE (Mt. Hood National Forest)
3 tent units, lake – no motors, swimming, fishing.
Northwest of Wamic. Cty 226 6 miles west, FSR 408/4800 10.5 miles
southwest, FSR 339/4860 10.3 miles northwest, FSR 21/3550 2 miles
northeast.

POST CAMP (Mt. Hood National Forest)
3 units, trailers to 22', fishing.
Southwest of Wamic. Cty 226 6 miles west, FSR 408/4800 11 miles
southwest, FSR 339/4860 2 miles northwest, FSR 468/4811 .7 miles
west.

WESTFIR

KIAHANIE (Willamette National Forest)
21 units, trailers okay, river, fishing.
Northeast of Westfir. FSR 19 19.3 miles northeast.

SKOOKUM CREEK (Willamette National Forest)
8 units, trailers okay, well, trails.
Northeast of Westfir. FSR 19 31.4 miles northeast, FSR 1957 3.7 miles
to campground.

WESTON

MOTTET (Umatilla National Forest)
9 units, trailers okay, stream.
East of Weston. State 204 17.5 miles east, FSR 64 2.1 miles east, FSR 20
.8 miles northeast, FSR 6403 9.1 miles northeast.

WHITE CITY

NORTH FORK (Rogue River National Forest)
7 tent units, stream, fishing, closed if without volunteer maintenance.
Northeast of White City. Cty 140 28.1 miles northeast, FSR 3706 1 mile
south.

WHITNEY

FOURTH CREEK (Wallowa-Whitman National Forest)
2 units, trailers okay, creek, trails.
South of Whitney. State 7 to Cty 507 4 miles south.

YACHATS

BIG CREEK (Siuslaw National Forest)
4 units, trailers to 18', stream.
Southeast of Yachats. US 101 10.7 miles south, FSR 57 6.4 miles east.
Narrow road.

LANHAM BIKE & HIKE (Siuslaw National Forest)
8 tent units, creek, fishing, hike-in.
South of Yachats. US 101 10 miles south, Trail 1373 .3 miles east.

TENMILE CREEK (Siuslaw National Forest)
4 unis, trailers to 18', stream, fishing, trail.
Southeast of Yachats. US 101 7.6 miles south, FSR 56 5 miles east.

Please send me the following books –

_____ copies of WASHINGTON FREE @ $9.95 each

_____ copies of OREGON FREE @ $9.95 each

_____ copies of FREE CAMPGROUNDS OF WASHINGTON &
OREGON @ $5.95 each

I have enclosed a check for $_____. (Please add $1.00 per book
to cover shipping costs.)

If VISA/MasterCard include:

Card # _____ Exp. Date _____

Signature _____

Name _____

Address _____

City/State/Zip _____

Send this order form to: Ki^2 Enterprises
P.O. Box 13322
Portland, Oregon 97213

Please send me the following books –

_____ copies of WASHINGTON FREE @ $9.95 each

_____ copies of OREGON FREE @ $9.95 each

_____ copies of FREE CAMPGROUNDS OF WASHINGTON &
OREGON @ $5.95 each

I have enclosed a check for $_____. (Please add $1.00 per book
to cover shipping costs.)

If VISA/MasterCard include:

Card # _____ Exp. Date _____

Signature _____

Name _____

Address _____

City/State/Zip _____

Send this order form to: Ki^2 Enterprises
P.O. Box 13322
Portland, Oregon 97213

INDEX

Water Skiing – 17, 18, 19, 21, 25, 30, 31, 35, 38, 44, 46, 53, 54, 62, 71.

Wilderness Access – 17, 18, 19, 20, 21, 23, 28, 29, 32, 34, 35, 42, 43, 44, 55, 56, 59, 64, 67, 74.